SENSORY YOGA FOR KIDS

Therapeutic Movement for Children of All Abilities

Britt Collins MS, OTR/L

Illustrations by Carly Jo Hougen

Sensory Yoga for Kids: Therapeutic Movement for Children of All Abilities

All marketing and publishing rights guaranteed to and reserved by:

Sensory World
A proud imprint of Future Horizons

721 W. Abram Street Arlington, TX 76013

Phone: 800•489•0727

Fax: 817•277•2270

Web: sensoryworld.com

Email: info@sensoryworld.com

ISBN: 9781935567486

Dedication

This book is dedicated to my amazing husband. Thank you for being my biggest support system and for always believing in me!

Disclaimer

I am an Occupational Therapist and am certified to teach yoga to children with special needs. I am not a physician nor have the ability to diagnose a child. This book offers information and guidance, but always check with your physician to determine if your child is healthy enough to practice yoga. Make sure you understand the yoga postures and/or are guided by a certified yoga instructor to help your child assume certain postures (especially if they have a physical disability). If you are working with an infant, make sure you have knowledge of yoga for infants or have been trained to work with small children.

Acknowledgements

There are many people who have provided incredible support to me during the process of writing this book. First and foremost, I would like to thank my wonderful husband. You are the best thing in my life. I also would like to thank my family for always believing I can reach the stars. I cannot offer enough thanks to the amazing professionals in my life, which include my amazing Special Education team at Aspen Crossing Elementary, who are becoming my second family. Thank you, Amber, for your support and for your interview for this book. You inspire me.

To the other amazing yogis I have met along the way, Molly, you are amazing, and thank you for helping me review the sequences and providing insightful information about traveling abroad and studying yoga in all parts of the world. Allison, my fellow OT, you are a bright light; thank you for the interviews and advice regarding yoga sequences. Thank you, Emily, for responding to all my crazy emails and deadlines and for your wonderful interview. You inspire all of us to keep living the best, healthiest lifestyle! Naseem, you are brilliant, and thank you for providing me with great research and thoughts on the yoga sequences. Heather, thank you for giving me your insight as an OT and yoga instructor. The work you do with children is wonderful.

Thank you to Sensory World, Jennifer and the editing team for making this book amazing!

Therapeutic Movement for Children of All Abilities

Sensory Yoga For Kids

WWW.SENSORYYOGAFORKIDS.COM

CONTENTS

INTRODUCTION

We all know that our bodies need movement to learn and regulate our nervous system. Many of us as adults take part in some form of exercise during our weekly activities to help us feel good; for example, walking, stretching, practicing yoga, lifting weights, swimming, running, or at least moving throughout our day from activity to activity. Some of us are not as diligent about exercising, but we cannot deny the research evidence that exercise several times a week is important to maintain a healthy heart, mind, and body. We also know that the use of calming strategies helps us when we are stressed. Things like deep breathing and taking a moment to stop and be still amid the chaos of life can help reduce stress and can change the way our brain processes anxiety and stress.

I am a pediatric Occupational Therapist (OT) who loves working with children, and I find that activities like yoga and mindfulness can be greatly beneficial to all the children I work with, regardless of their abilities and disabilities.

As an OT, I am lucky enough to get natural exercise in my day-to-day job. Does this mean I shouldn't still go to the gym or to the studio? No! But do I always? Of course not—I am human and have a busy life and completely understand what it means to be exhausted. That being said, I know that I should do as much as I can for my body and mind to get myself to the gym or studio or outside. Yoga can become more of a lifestyle for you and your family. Practicing yoga on a regular basis can help you learn how to regulate your breathing; maintain a calm, happy and regulated nervous system; and, of course, helps build strength and flexibility. It is also important to strive for a "mindful" life. Mindfulness involves paying attention to the present moment and remaining aware of your current body and breath. Mindfulness can include a focus on what you hear around you, how you are breathing, your body and movement and healthy eating. Yoga, therapeutic movement and mindfulness all go hand in hand.

Children in general are usually good at exercising naturally. Aren't we always telling them, "Stop running through the house!" or "Go outside to play that game!" Many parents put their child into activities such as dance, baseball, swim lessons, gymnastics and karate. These are great activities for your child to participate in for more reasons than just exercise. These activities help them with social skills, learning to play as part of a team, giving them movement, which helps regulate their nervous system (see more in Chapter 1).

Now why do we think yoga or therapeutic movement could be beneficial for us and our children? Well, it helps improve movement, strength, breathing and more, and children need this stimulation. In this book I will take you through a journey of understanding what sensory processing is, how it affects regulation, how yoga helps with sensory regulation, and how to adapt yoga to meet your child's specific needs. We will also discuss mindfulness and how to use therapeutic movement at school and in the classroom.

Deep breathing, meditation, massage, and yoga have been identified as the four complementary and alternative medicine therapies used by adults in the United States that have significantly increased from 2002 to 2007, with deep breathing and yoga identified as the third and fourth most commonly used interventions with children during the same time period (Barnes, Bloom, and Nahin, 2008).

Introduction

All of these aspects can become part of your lifestyle, one moment at a time. These strategies, ideas, and techniques will hopefully help you better yourself as a parent/caregiver, therapist or teacher and improve the lives of your child or the children with whom you work.

CHAPTER 1:

WHAT IS SENSORY PROCESSING? HOW DOES IT AFFECT OUR BODIES?

Easy Pose

Chapter 1: What is Sensory Processing?

You have heard me say, "Regulate their nervous system." Now, what does that mean? In OT terms, this phrase refers to finding your child's just-right state for learning and functioning.

Each one of us has a nervous system we have to manage every day. Some of us are naturally calm and collected, and others are more anxious, "on the go" or busy all day long. No matter what your nature is, you know certain things can rev up your nervous system and other things can calm your system down. I know that I need a calm, quiet environment to focus and write this book. Others might like music or the TV on for background noise. Most of you as mothers and fathers learn how to work in a busy loud environment if you have children at home, because they can be loud, run around, and constantly ask questions, etc. Some parents describe this as functioning in chaos.

A yoga teacher once told me that, even in the chaos of life, we can find respite in taking just a few slow deep breaths and being still for a moment to reset our system and then continue our day.

Our children also need certain tools and strategies to regulate their nervous systems. Such tools could include calming music to help them sleep as you rock them, or it could be getting outside and running around playing for 30-45 minutes before dinner so they will sit still and finish a meal. We all need something different, and in this book I will talk about ways to help each type of nervous system find its just-right state!

Sensory Processing (you may have heard this as Sensory Integration or SI) is the brain's ability to take in external and internal information, process it effectively and produce an appropriate motor and behavioral response.

Children and adults who have Sensory Processing Disorder (SPD) struggle with the ability to process that information from their senses and have an appropriate motor or behavioral response.

We have 8 sensory systems that affect our overall regulation:

1. Taste (Gustatory System)
2. Touch (Tactile System)
3. Smell (Olfactory System)
4. Sight (Visual System)
5. Sound (Auditory System)
6. Vestibular System: This system governs your balance. It tells you whether your head is right side up or upside down. This system allows us to know how fast we are moving and in what direction. The fluid in the inner ear helps us maintain our balance and coordination.
7. Proprioceptive System: How our body is positioned and moving in space (body awareness)
8. Interoception: Our sense of internal organs, pain, temperature, hunger, bladder and bowel sensations

Chapter 1: What is Sensory Processing?

Excerpt from Sensory Parenting: The Elementary Years[1]

Dr. Lucy Jane Miller with the SPD foundation based in Denver, CO, is one of our leading researchers in the field for SPD. According to Miller et al. (2007), "There are at least six subtypes of SPD and many people have a combination of more than one. With eight sensory systems and six or more subtypes, there are over 8 factorial x 6 factorial or 29,030,400 possible combinations. No wonder children with SPD can look so different." This means that not only does almost every one of you who is reading this book have a sensory sensitivity, but also, your brain processes sensory input in a unique way. We all have different responses to sensory information.

The first category is Sensory Modulation Disorder (SMD), which is then broken down into 3 subtypes:

1. Sensory Over-Responsivity (SOR)
2. Sensory Under-Responsivity (SUR)
3. Sensory Craving (SC) (sometimes called Sensory Seeking)

Sensory Over-Responsivity (SOR) occurs during a sensory experience when the brain interprets the information too easily or too intensely and can send the body into a fight, flight or freeze response. Children experiencing these reactions feel things too fast and avoid certain activities. They may cover their ears in response to loud noises, resist movement, or withdraw from being touched. Here is how some children may experience being SOR in each sensory domain. The part of the brain that processes this fight, flight or freeze response is called the amygdala. This small part of your brain helps process and control emotions, and when we trigger a fear or a fight response, it can take over, and then sometimes we forget how to use our prefrontal cortex to make a good positive decision (see more about the amygdala in Chapter 12). A child facing SOR may exhibit the following behavior in each sensory area:

1. Vestibular: Does not engage in climbing, swinging, or spinning activities
2. Tactile: Avoids touching sticky or gooey things
3. Auditory: May get disorganized in noisy environments like a mall or sports arena
4. Visual: Is uncomfortable in the sun unless wearing sunglasses
5. Olfactory: Shies away from smells such as dinner cooking
6. Taste: Has a small set of foods they are willing to eat
7. Proprioceptive: May not like to feel pressure on their feet or legs; refuses to jump, hop, or skip
8. Interoception: May feel small stomach-aches too intensely (and as a result are in the nurse's office frequently).

Sensory Under-Responsiveness (SUR) occurs during a sensory experience when the brain is slow to interpret the information presented. Children experiencing this response may appear withdrawn or self-absorbed or rarely start interactions with other people. They may show poor body awareness due to the under-responsiveness to tactile and deep-pressure input. This can make them look clumsy, slow and lethargic. These children may not notice when they get hurt or when the stove is too hot to touch, because their systems are not registering fast enough or high enough. These children also may appear self-absorbed and withdrawn. Here are ways that a child may face SUR in each of the sensory domains.

Chapter 1: What is Sensory Processing?

1. Vestibular: Does not engage in physical activities and prefers sedentary tasks
2. Tactile: May not notice if he or she gets hurt or bumped
3. Auditory: Doesn't respond to his or her name being called; may hum to him- or herself while working on a task
4. Visual: Loses place when reading, complain of eyes being tired
5. Olfactory: Does not notice strong odors that others notice
6. Taste: Does not notice or care if foods are spicy or bland
7. Proprioceptive: Slumps in chair or leans on walls, may have weak muscles
8. Interoception: Has potty accidents, is unaware of when he or she is hungry; has poor body awareness

Sensory Craving (SC)/Sensory Seeking (SS) disorders occur when a child craves certain sensory input over and over again. He or she wants to be constantly moving and often crashes into things or jumps. Some of these children can be overly affectionate and invade others' space without realizing it. These children are almost addicted to the sensation they are craving and can't get enough of it. The following are ways that a child may experience SC in each of the sensory systems.

1. Vestibular: constantly craves the sensation of spinning, running, or moving; loves extreme fast-moving activities, such as ice skating, jumping off high towers, riding roller coasters, and skateboarding fast.
2. Tactile: Wants to be always touching other people or objects, always wants to put things in the mouth or chew holes in clothing
3. Auditory: Constantly makes noises to self or talks loudly, enjoys noisy environments

4. Visual: Likes to watch things spin or move more than same-age peers, likes brightly colored objects
5. Olfactory: Wants to smell everything he or she can, even non-food objects
6. Taste: Craves strong flavors: spicy, salty, sour
7. Proprioceptive: Is constantly jumping, crashing, bumping into things, giving hard high fives or hugs, likes tight-fitted clothing

Some children seek input to their nervous system to stay regulated. Many researchers vary on how they describe this subtype of SPD. It can be called Sensory Seeking or Sensory Craving, This is described as part of the regulation process in which children may be over- or under-responding to a sense and need to get more input to that sensory system to stay regulated.

For example, you see a child who is constantly touching everything, putting things in his mouth, running around and being unable to sit still. Is this because he is trying to get more input to his sensory system to make sense of it all? Is this because he is dysregulated and trying to figure out how to find his just-right state for learning? What we know is that we see these types of children who are constantly trying to receive input into their nervous system, and the more they seek, the more dysregulated they can become. We need to help provide them sensory-rich activities to help calm and regulate their nervous system, and yoga can be one such tool to help them.

The second category of SPD is Sensory Based Motor Disorder (SBMD), which is broken down into two subtypes: Postural Disorder and Dyspraxia.

Children with Postural Control Disorder show poor core strength and decreased endurance. It is difficult for these children to stabilize their trunk and co-contract the muscles to help maintain their balance. Children who display weakness in this area of SPD have difficulty performing efficient movements and show poor body awareness, especially in the tactile and proprioceptive systems. They may exhibit a poor sitting or standing position, and their bodies work harder to maintain their posture, which can lead to fatigue.

A child who is struggling with this area of difficulty may demonstrate decreased ability to climb up a ladder or onto an uneven surface, like a swing. She has to concentrate harder on maintaining her core stability, thus making simple tasks like stepping onto an escalator or stepping off the curb of the sidewalk more difficult.

Praxis is broken down into three parts: coming up with an idea (ideation), planning a sequence for the task and then performing the motor task (motor planning). Children who have dyspraxia may have difficulty getting dressed, cutting out a shape or coming up with new ideas to play a game with their peers. They may be accident-prone, have poor ball-playing skills or have difficulty with fine motor skills. Sometimes these children prefer sedentary activities or try to avoid the motor tasks by talking up the idea or fantasy play but never acting out the idea.

Yoga and therapeutic movement can also benefit core strength, coordination, balance, sequencing of movements and more.

The third category of SPD is Sensory Discrimination Disorder (SDD), which can affect any of the eight sensory systems.

Being able to discriminate something means you can take in the information and attribute meaning to it. Children with SDD have a "poor ability to interpret information or give meaning to the specific qualities of the stimuli" (Miller 2011). They may have trouble distinguishing between letters like b and d. It may be difficult for them to reach into their pocket and pick out the paper clip and not the penny. Sometimes it takes these children more time to process certain sensory stimuli. This is good to know about our children with SPD, but we will not create a specific yoga sequence for this subtype.

No matter what behavior or sensory challenge you are facing with your particular child, there are great benefits to their participation in yoga or other types of therapeutic movement to help regulate their nervous system. There are movements that can calm them down and others that can rev them up to find that just-right state for learning and functioning.

See Chapter 5 for our specific yoga sequences to help these kiddos.

CHAPTER 2:

BACKGROUND ON YOGA

Child's Pose

Chapter 2: Background on Yoga

The history of yoga started more than 5,000 years ago. The origins of yoga are speculated to pre-date Indian traditions, and many religions like Hinduism, Buddhism and Janism later adopted many yoga techniques as part of their worship practices. The literal meaning of yoga is "to add," "to join," "to unite," or "to attach."

The two main focuses of yoga are Hatha yoga and Raja yoga, and there are many more forms of yoga practice. One of the earliest texts shows that a scholar started yoga as early as the 1st or 2nd century B.C. Yoga became more popular in the United States most likely around the 1960s, and research has shown that yoga can benefit cancer recovery, mental disability, asthma, back pain and heart disease. Any who practice yoga know that there are millions of more reasons why yoga can benefit both children and adults.[2]

The yoga system was built on three main structures: exercise, breathing, and meditation. Exercise benefits the body's total health and strength, breathing is the source of life for the body, and meditation helps quiet the mind and facilitates healing from daily stress.

Hatha yoga is described as "The physical movements and postures, plus breathing techniques. This is what most people associate with yoga practice."

Raja yoga is "Called the 'royal road,' because it incorporates exercise and breathing practice with meditation and study, producing a well-rounded individual."[3]

Yoga and Religion

Yoga is not a religion; it does not have a set of beliefs or worship of a god. "The core of yoga's philosophy is that everything is supplied from within the individual." [4]

People who practice yoga may also be religious, as this practice does not interfere with one's beliefs. Some people consider themselves to be spiritual people, and yoga can help support that belief. One can also practice yoga and not consider oneself religious or spiritual. Yoga can be about a healthy mind, body and spirit and providing a quiet place to strengthen, stretch, and be calm.

Yoga and Children

Yoga classes for children are popping up all around the United States and in other countries. It has become a popular desire for parents to find a yoga class for their children. Parents may seek yoga for their child for a variety of reasons, including teaching them discipline, learning calming techniques, giving them a sense of confidence, improving body strength and balance and coordination, and improving focus and attention. Research also has shown us that yoga benefits can include regulating mood, improving behaviors and decreasing anxiety and stress in adults and children. Anyone who has practiced yoga regularly knows that these things can help. This is just one more tool parents can use with their children who have special needs.

For children who may have a specific special need, a parent may look for a specific yoga instructor who is trained to work with children with special needs. People with both mental and physical disabilities can enjoy yoga, but parents should make sure that the instructor is familiar with their children's specific needs.

Yoga for Typically Developing Children

Any child can benefit from the yoga sequences we have discussed in this book, not just those children with special needs. Any sibling, friend, cousin, etc., can also take part in the yoga sequences, and many times it's motivating for those children with special needs to have someone perform the yoga poses with them.

Standing Forward Bend

As mentioned before with any child, you want to make sure they are being safe and their body is in good alignment and that you only push them as far as their body will allow. Everyone, even us as adults, can benefit from all parts of yoga, and this can be an amazing experience for us to share with our children.

Yoga for Infants and Toddlers Under the Age of 2

Baby yoga is very beneficial to a baby, and you can perform it with a newborn infant as long as you have been trained, practice yoga yourself regularly, or are being guided by a trained children's yoga instructor or OT/PT therapist. Babies love to be stretched, massaged, moved in various positions and touched.

Cobra Pose

Yoga can provide all of those amazing sensations, but you must make sure it's safe for your infant and that he or she is healthy enough to practice yoga with you. If your baby has any medical issues (g-tubes, seizures, prematurity, heart conditions, lung conditions, or any other physical medical challenge), check with your pediatrician and specialists to see if you can safely practice with your baby.

Make sure you move slowly and gently, and watch your baby's facial expressions at all times. It should not be painful or upset them in any way. Infant massage can also be a wonderful tool to use with your infant or toddler.

Please realize that the sequences listed in our chapters below are for children ages 2 years and up. If your child is chronologically older (i.e. 4

years, etc.) but is developmentally functioning around a 1 to 2 year old, again make sure they are cleared by their physician to take part in the yoga sequences in the following chapters.

What Does Yoga Teach Us?

- Bodies – physical postures and exercise (called asanas) help bring strength and flexibility to our bodies. There are both active and passive asanas, and both benefit your mind and body for different reasons.
- Active poses help build strength, flexibility, and muscle tone; help move energy throughout the body; and activate the brain and nervous system.
- Passive poses are mostly for meditation and deep relaxation. These are typically done at the end of your yoga practice for 10 to 20 minutes.
- This also helps improve body awareness and helps children learn to listen to their bodies. What is my body telling me? Am I sick, tired, happy, sad, mad? What can I do about these feelings?
- Breath -- Breathing is a crucial part of life, but do we take slow deep breaths effectively? Teaching a child how to breathe slowly and deeply (called pranayama) can bring them calmness and energy. "Pranayama is the formal practice of controlling our breath. We try to improve breathing patterns in children who are chest breathers to use a more diaphragmatic breathing technique. This type of breathing helps decrease stress and anxiety. (See Chapter 4 for more breathing techniques.) Deep breathing helps us relax by de-activating the sympathetic nervous system (SNS), which produces stress

hormones and activates our parasympathetic nervous system (PNS) instead, which then helps lower blood pressure, decrease heart rate and relaxes us.[5]

The best way to learn pranayama is with a trained yoga teacher.

I like to think of the vagus nerve as the body's engine of resilience and affiliation. Located in the medulla oblongata of the brainstem, the vagus nerve is an essential part of parasympathetic nervous system (PNS) and mediates changes in heart rate (Porges, Doussard-Roosevelt, & Mait, 1994). Vagal tone refers to the activity of this nerve and regulates the rest and digest state of much of the body's internal organ systems, including the lungs and heart (Porges et al., 1994). Children and adults alike can strengthen their vagal tone by taking slow, diaphragmatic breaths—usually 5 to 6 breaths per minute. (excerpt from interview with Naseem Rashadi; see page 168)

- Energy (called prana) – Helps us feel more relaxed, focused and motivated. Prana is our "vital life force."
- Balance – Teaches us how to coordinate both sides of our body and strengthening our core muscles. When we use the right and left sides of our bodies, it makes both sides of our brain communicate through the corpus callosum, which presents many benefits to our children in learning, reading, and bilateral coordination activities like tying shoes and riding a bike.
- Being Still – Teaches us how to quiet the mind, focus, and concentrate, while not letting your mind wander.

- Taking care of ourselves – Teaches children how to take care of their health including diet, exercise, and sleep.

Mantras/Chanting

Chanting mantras can be beneficial for children, as it combines sound, breath, and rhythm together. The vibrations of the sounds can help regulate a child, and some children like to feel their throat or chest vibrate. Many children on the autism spectrum will vocalize various sounds repetitively, and it is thought that this feels good to them inside.

In schools, you want to be cautious about chanting the sound "OM" or other Sanskrit words or prayers. It is fine if you use this in your yoga practice, but we have to be sensitive to all of our children and their beliefs. You want to make sure that if you are practicing yoga poses with children in school, you have permission from their parents to make this a part of their therapy or classroom sensory breaks.

You can chant different sounds and words with kids; this can be fun or serious, but make sure you are being respectful of your environment and what type of setting you are working in.

You can even play music that has a strong drumbeat to help provide a solid rhythm while practicing yoga with your child or children you are working with. I enjoy using David & Steve Gordon *Sacred Earth Drums* music. This is grounding for children any time, not just during yoga practice.

Mindfulness

Mindfulness is defined as a mental state achieved by focusing one's awareness on the present moment, while calmly acknowledging and accepting one's feelings, thoughts, and bodily sensations. This is a therapeutic technique that involves living in the moment and making every moment just as important as your last. Everyone thinks about the past, and we learn from our past just as we dream about the future. These are great experiences to have, but I want to encourage you to be present; think about how you feel right now. What does your body feel like where you are sitting and reading this book? Take a minute, close your eyes and just take a few breaths and think only about your breathing.

Mindfulness involves paying attention to your breath. Mindful breathing is being aware of your current breath. Don't change how you are breathing, just take note. Feel where you are breathing. Through the nostrils? In your chest? In your lungs? Or in your belly? Now you have done that, open your eyes and allow your brain to take all of this information in you are reading and learning and process it.

Our minds wander, and we think about all the things we need to be doing (i.e. making a grocery list, preparing for work, picking up the kids from soccer, oh don't forget to make the costumes for the kids' school play, feeding the dog, and this list goes on and on)! I personally have an ADD-type of brain and find it difficult to slow down, stop trying to think about everything at once, and just focus on my breath. I am learning more and more every day about how to be in the present and listen to my body and focus on my breath. This has been helpful for me to deal with any pain, stress, anxiety, etc., I might be feeling from my personal life or my work life. This is an ongoing practice for me as it will be for you and your child you are working with.

According to Kristen Race, PhD., Founder of Mindful Life™, Mindful Body, Mindful Listening, Mindful Breathing, and Mindful Eating are all important parts of her program. She created a curriculum for schools to train their teachers and staff in bringing mindfulness into the classroom. See Chapter 11: "Yoga in Schools" for more information regarding her program.

Mindfulness can improve our:

- Awareness
- Focus
- It helps change our brain
- Reduces stress and depression
- Helps build relationships

A study found that after 8 weeks of training, practicing mindfulness boosts our immune system's ability to fight off illness.[6]

Mindfulness directly relates to the brain and how it functions.

CHAPTER 3:

BEFORE PRACTICING YOGA WITH A CHILD

Butterfly Pose

The yoga practice is a 'practice for a life,' a tool that the child can turn to on the playground, in the classroom or in any stressful situation. In this sense, practicing on the yoga mat becomes a symbolic space for a child to explore, challenge, and better acquire learning strategies, not only for the yoga shapes, but also for all the kinds of shapes and situations that the child will encounter off the mat and in life."

—Naseem Rashedi

Tools for Practicing Yoga

- A yoga mat or a towel (something to define the space for a child)
- Folded blanket
- Water bottle
- Comfortable clothes
- Possibly a block
- Calming music or even fun music, depending on the child
- A quiet space

What You Need to Do as the Adult First

Before you, as a parent, practice yoga with your child, you should have a basic understanding of yoga. You need to know the various body positions and postures so you can help your child appropriately. If you are not comfortable yet with your own body and yoga, take a few classes to find what best suites you, and then make sure your child is healthy enough to practice yoga. You can also have a yoga instructor work directly with your child, but make sure that, if your child has special needs, the instructor knows how to work with children with special needs. It takes a wealth of knowledge to understand how to work with children with physical, mental or emotional needs and yoga can be a powerful tool to help all children.

If you are a therapist (OT, PT, SLP, Mental Health Provider, Special Education teacher, etc.) you probably already have a lot of knowledge about the children you work with. Using yoga as a technique and tool with the children you see can be very beneficial. You as a practitioner should still practice yoga yourself and learn and understand how it affects your body, mind and spirit so you can best support the children that you are serving.

If you are already a trained yoga instructor and you want to specifically teach children with special needs, there are many courses offered not only in kids' yoga, but also specifically designed for children with special needs. This is beneficial for you as a yoga instructor to help you understand the variety of needs and abilities of a child you might encounter. Please see the resource section of this book for further resources.

Children are made to sit still for much of their day while in school or in other environments that require learning. However, they need to move to learn. Yoga for kids can be fun and even a little silly. Yes, we want them to be safe and learn how to move through poses/asanas effectively, but we call certain poses silly names that make it more child-friendly. You will see that in the book, there are kid-friendly names for poses and some alternate names you might be more familiar with. Illustrations of all the poses will be provided so you know exactly how you and your child's body position should be. Yoga can be very calming and serious, and if your child has good concentration and focus, then by all means, have them quietly move through poses or help them to do so. I find when working with my toddlers and young children, it's easier to keep their focus if I sing a silly song or pretend to be an animal and move into that pose. I also find that sometimes children need to stand and "get their sillies out" and then get back to the poses I am trying to get them to imitate. Children who may have physical limitations and may not be running off their mat can still benefit from you singing to them and engaging them in the fun part of yoga.

Once children learn the discipline of focus and attention, you can increase their ability to sit and be still and quiet and calm their minds. Meditation and relaxation is difficult for most adults, so children will learn over time the more often they practice.

Getting Your Space Ready for Yoga!

If you will practice at home or in a school, it's nice to have a clear, clean space with yoga mats to practice with your child. You want to make sure the lights are not too bright; natural light from windows might be best. If you do not have access to enough windows, a floor lamp with low lighting is good. Provide enough light to see but not to be overbearing, especially when the child is lying on his back. You can play soft calming music or even fun, silly music if that is the theme you are going for with your yoga practice that day. Some music I like is most is anything by Enya, *Sacred Earth Drums* by David and Steve Gordon, *Mantra* by Jane Winther, and anything else that appeals to you and your child.

Yoga is traditionally practiced barefoot, but some children prefer to leave their socks on. That is okay, as long as they are not slipping and hurting themselves when moving through poses.

Start by engaging with the child/children you are working with. If you are a therapist and are new to this child, you want to find common ground with them and build a trust relationship. It's great to laugh with children, but a child might also like to start with grounding drum beat music or chanting to get them engaged. Each child is different and you need to know your audience.

Keep your voice calm but happy, and smile so when the children look to your face, they are comforted by your smile.

CHAPTER 4:

YOGA POSES AND THEIR BENEFITS

As follows, we will describe each pose and summarize its benefits. Later these poses will be put into various suggested sequences to help meet the specific needs of your child. This chapter intends to define and describe each pose individually so you can have all poses organized in one place. As you read, you will find which areas of challenge most affect your child that particular day or time and can then use that sequence of poses to help your child.

Breathing Techniques

- *Alternate Nostril Breathing*
  Sit comfortably in Easy Pose or kneeling position. Start by placing your left hand on your thigh with the thumb and index finger touching. Then take your right hand up to your face. Your right thumb is gently touching your right nostril and your right ring finger is gently touching the left nostril. You are not using your index and middle finger; they can gently rest in between your eyebrows or tuck them in. Close your right nostril with your thumb and inhale through your left nostril for 4 counts and then close left nostril and open right nostril. Exhale out of the right nostril for 4 counts, inhale through the right nostril and then exhale through the left nostril. Try this up to 8 rounds if you can. If a child restricts their breath then stop. This should be easy for the child.

- *Bumblebee Breath*

  Hold a flower in your hand or a pretend flower, breath in through your nose and then hum as you breath out making a buzzing bee noise. Try making higher-pitched buzzing, then lower-pitched buzzing.

- *Bellows Breath*

  When starting Bellows Breath, start by sitting with your spine straight in an effortless posture. You can do this while sitting cross-legged on the floor with a blanket underneath your sitting bones, or you can sit in a chair with your back straight. Both the inhalation and exhalation are forceful and have equal emphasis (you can hear it out your nose as your stomach presses in and out). Sometimes it is nice to start by placing your hands on your stomach to feel your breath going in and out. Each inhalation and exhalation is at the rate of 1 per second, so you start out slowly with 10 breaths. Then take a few resting breaths and then try 10 more breaths. You can speed up your bellows breath and then slow it down again at the end. Make sure the child does not report or look lightheaded when breathing quickly this way until she is used to practicing this.

- *Volcano Breath*

  Stand in Mountain Pose, bring hands to heart center, inhale reach arms up, then as you exhale bend forward and exhale all your breath making an Ahhh sound like an erupting volcano. Repeat 2-3 times.

- *Mindful Breathing*

  Mindfulness is discussed more in Chapter 12, but I want to describe it here as well, because it will show up in some of the yoga sequences as a beginning activity for increasing awareness, grounding, calming and regulating the nervous system. Mindful breathing is being aware of your current breath, feeling how you normally breathe and paying attention to how your breath feels. Is it warm or cool; do you feel it coming in through the nostrils, down the throat and into your lungs? Do not change your breath; just be aware of how you are breathing, while either sitting in a chair or on the floor in a mindful body position.[7]

Eye Exercises

There are many benefits that yoga provides for our eyes, and you can do eye exercises to help strengthen and rejuvenate them. One is to sit in Easy Pose, relax your body and take several deep breaths. Then rub your hands together several times, creating heat in your hands, and then place the palms of your hands over your eyes so that all you see is dark. Relax and allow the heat from your palms to relax your eyes. Hold this position for 10-15 seconds.

Another great eye exercise is to look straight ahead and then pretend there is a clock in front of you. Think of looking at 12, 3, 6, 9 and back to 12 (without moving your head) and then to 3, 6, 9 and back to 12. Then repeat in the opposite direction. If you are working with a young child, you can sit in front of him with a pencil that has a cute eraser on the end of it and have him hold his head still and follow your pencil through the clock positions. This helps strengthen the eye muscles. After doing this exercise, practice the palm-to-eyes position again to relax them and keep them shut for 10-15 seconds.

Alphabetical List of Yoga Poses

When practicing with children, we want to make sure they are in good alignment, but we know they are wiggly little creatures, and this can sometimes be hard. Try to model good posture positions for them, and if they are young or have a physical disability, you will help them move into and out of the poses safely. The descriptions will help you know how to assume the pose and then assist those who need it. If possible, its best to allow the child to imitate you unless you are worried she will hurt herself, then please physically help cue her into the correct position. If you are unsure of any poses and the safety of them with your child, skip that pose and ask a professional yoga instructor how to help guide you.

1. Bridge Pose

Lie on your back, bend your knees, and place your feet flat on the floor. Bring your heels closer to your buttocks and extend your arms down by your side. Then, when you are ready, lift your hips off the ground slowly while breathing.

 If you are assisting a child in this pose, sit to the side of him and help hold his feet on the ground while slowly lifting underneath his lower back/hips. If his feet lifts or slides, then lower his hand on his back so you are not pulling him up too high. Be careful you are not hurting his neck or that, if he is doing this alone, his head and neck are aligned with the body.

Benefits:

- Improves circulation
- Improves digestion
- Stretches neck, chest, hips and spine
- Strengthens hamstrings and buttocks
- Reduces headaches

2. Bow Pose

Lie on your tummy, arms down by your side, palms facing up. Take 2-3 slow deep breaths. As you exhale, bend your knees, bringing your heels as close to your bottom as you can. Reach back and grab your ankles. If this is as far as you can go, that is fine; if you can go further, inhale and lift your heels away from your bottom, pulling your chest and head up. Make sure your shoulders are relaxed. Be sure to keep breathing.

Alternative poses: Half bow – You can help a child by helping her reach her arms back to hold her ankles, or you can bend her knees and gently hold them for her while she is lying on her tummy. Be careful not to overstretch the quadriceps muscles if they are tight.

You can also just bend one leg at a time while the child is lying on her tummy and stretch their quadriceps until she is ready to go to the next step.

Do not do this yourself or with a child if you have lower back pain.

Benefits:
- Improves circulation
- Improves digestion
- Strengthens the back and increases flexibility in the back
- Stretches the entire front of the body, including neck and chest
- Improves function of liver, pancreas and large and small intestines

3. Butterfly (Bound Angle Pose)

Start by sitting on your buttocks with both legs straight out in front of you. Then bring both legs in, with the soles of the feet touching. You can have a folded blanket underneath your buttocks if needed for comfort. Bring your heels as close to your pelvis as you can, and relax your knees as they fall to the sides. They do not have to touch the floor. If this is an uncomfortable pose to hold for long, you can place folded blankets under each knee to make this more relaxing. Make sure your back is straight.

Be cautious if you have a knee injury.

Benefits:

- Improves circulation
- Helps with anxiety and fatigue
- Stimulates abdominal organs
- Stretches groin and thighs

4. Cat/Cow Pose

Begin on your hands and knees with a neutral back (table pose), then take a breath in, sink your tummy down towards the floor, bring your head up and look forward. Then as you exhale, round your back, tuck your tailbone, and look down towards the floor. Continue cat/cow stretches following your breathing for 5-7 breaths.

Benefits:

- Strengthens and stretches the spine
- Stretches tummy, hips and back
- Creates emotional balance
- Massages the internal organs

5. Chair Pose

Start in Mountain Pose, inhale, reach the arms up, and either connect the hands or face the palms in. As you exhale, bend your knees like you are sitting in a chair and try to get your thighs parallel to the floor. Your knees will slightly reach over your toes. Activate your thigh muscles and squeeze your shoulder blades slightly.

Take caution with this pose if you have low blood pressure or a headache

Benefits:

- Strengthens thighs, calves, ankles and back

- Helps build core strength
- Helps work on balance
- Stretches shoulders and chest
- Stimulates abdominal organs and heart

6. Child's Pose

Kneel and sit back on your heels, then slightly open your knees so your big toes are touching behind you. Lean forward so your forehead is touching the ground and reach your arms out in front of you. You can also relax your arms by your side. This is a resting pose.

Benefits:

- Stretches the spine
- Releases tension in the back
- Calms the mind (which reduces stress) and encourages strong breathing
- Improves circulation, which reduces headaches

7. Cobra Pose

Lie on your stomach on the floor with your legs stretched out with the tops of the feet on the floor. Bring your hands up by your shoulders, keep your elbows close to your body, and then inhale and gently press your torso up only as far as your lower back will allow. You can press up to where you have a soft bend in the elbows. Keep your pelvic bones on the floor and try to relax your buttocks. Hold for 10-15 seconds and exhale, coming back to the floor.

Do not do this pose if you have a back injury, carpal tunnel syndrome or a headache Alternatives for this could be Sphinx Pose—see below.

Benefits:
- Stimulates abdominal muscles
- Opens heart and lungs
- Lengthens the spine and strengthens the back
- Therapeutic for asthma
- Stretches chest, shoulders and back
- Strengthens arms
- Increases flexibility
- Improves digestion
- Elevates mood

8. Crescent Moon Pose

Start in Mountain Pose, inhale and reach overhead. Interlock your fingers, keeping your index fingers pointed toward the sky. Exhale and stretch over to the right, pressing your hip opposite towards the left. Hold this for 10-15 seconds, then straighten the back to standing, and bring hands to heart center. Repeat on the other side.

If you are helping a child do this, make sure you gently guide him through the arch and prevent him from bending forward. Do not push him past his comfort zone.

You may also do this pose seated for those children who have physical disabilities or those children who struggle with standing balance.

Benefits:
- Improves balance and core strength
- Increases circulation
- Improves flexibility of spine
- Promotes kidney function

9. Downward Dog Pose

Start in tabletop, and on an exhale, press your legs back and lift your hips up. Keep your knees slightly bent at first and stretch out your hamstrings and calf muscles. Then slowly try to deepen the stretch by pressing your hips back and heels closer to the floor. Your feet do not have to be together. Start slowly and work toward holding it for longer periods.

Since this is an intense inversion posture, come back to child's pose if you feel lightheaded or dizzy. Be cautious if you have wrist injury or blood pressure issues. Since this is an inversion posture, it can be stimulating, so be careful with a child who you are trying to get to sleep.

Benefits:
- Energizes the body
- Stretches hamstrings, calves, shoulders and upper back
- Strengthens arms and legs
- Therapeutic for sinusitis and asthma
- Relieves back pain, insomnia and fatigue
- Reduces stress and calms the brain

10. Easy Pose

Sit on the floor or on a folded blanket. Cross your legs and flex your feet underneath you. Try to sit like this during a few breaths, and then uncross and re-cross your legs the opposite way. Sit with your back straight up as though a string is pulling you up from the top of your head.

Benefits:
- Is a good starting pose for children to practice their breathing techniques
- Calms the body
- Strengthens the back

11. Extended Cat Pose

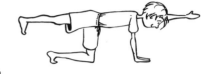

Start in Table Top, and after a few cat/cow stretches, go back to neutral spine, then reach out your right arm and your left leg. Hold this for 5-10 seconds while breathing. Bring your arms and legs back to Table Top, and now try the opposite side, with the left arm and right leg.

Benefits:
- Provides core strengthening
- Uses opposite sides of the body to help with bilateral coordination
- Prepares body for balancing postures
- Lengthens spine, arms and legs

12. Fish Pose

Lie on your back with your knees bent. Inhale and bring your hands underneath your buttocks, with palms down. Make sure your arms and elbows are close to your side. While inhaling, press your forearms and elbows into the floor and lift your chest. Depending on your flexibility, either the back of your head or the crown of your head will be touching the floor. You may keep your knees bent if you are learning this pose, and to reach a more advanced level, you may straighten your legs. There should not be much pressure on your head.

Do not do this pose if you have a neck injury, blood pressure issues or headaches.

Benefits:
- Stretches and opens chest and shoulders
- Stimulates the thyroid gland and improves immune system
- Circulates blood
- Helps with back pain
- Helps with constipation, fatigue and anxiety

13. Happy Baby Pose

Lie on your back, and while exhaling, bring your knees up to your chest. Inhale and grab onto the outsides of your feet and bring your feet out slightly towards your armpits.

Take caution if you are pregnant or have knee or ankle injuries or tight hips

Benefits:
- Helps relieve stress and fatigue
- Stretches inner thigh
- Stretches spine and relaxes the lower back

14. Head to Knee Forward-bend Pose

Sit on the floor with both legs straight out in front of you. Sit on a blanket under your bottom if needed. Bend right knee in resting your foot on the inside of your left thigh. Reach up high and inhale. As you exhale, reach down to your left foot, maintaining the flexed foot position. Only go as far as your body allows. Repeat this on the other side.

Benefits:
- Stimulates liver and kidneys
- Stretches shoulders and upper back and hamstring
- Helps improve digestion
- Helps with insomnia, anxiety and fatigue

15. Knee to Chest Pose

Lie on your back and bring both knees into your chest and hug them tight. Then use your right arm to hold the right shin and straighten the left leg to the floor. Bring your right knee into your chest, hold 5-10 seconds, then move it slightly towards your armpit and hold it for 5-10 seconds. Then bring your knee back into the middle and straighten your leg. Repeat on the opposite leg. You can also bring both knees into your chest and squeeze them close.

Benefits:
- Helps with gas, bloating and digestion
- The right side is the ascending colon
- The left side is the descending colon

16. Legs up the Wall Pose

Lie on your back and scoot your buttocks as close to the wall as possible. You may place a blanket underneath your hips for support. Raise your legs up the wall and relax.

Benefits:
- Gently stretches hamstrings and calves
- Helps relieve stress and anxiety
- Calms the mind
- Helps relax the lower back
- Is therapeutic for headaches and blood pressure issues

17. Lion Pose

Sit on your knees. Sit up nice and tall with hands on your knees, or you can lean forward with hands right in front of you on the floor. Inhale, and while exhaling, stick your tongue out and make a hard sound with your breath AHHH like a lion roar.

Benefits:
- Provides stress relief
- Stimulates the throat and vocal cords (great for children working on speech language)
- Relieves tension in face and chest

18. Lunge Pose

You can transition into this pose from Downward Facing Dog Pose or from Standing Forward Bend Pose. If you are in Downward Facing Dog, step up with your right foot and keep your knee directly over your ankle. You can stay with your hands down on the floor or come up with your chest and place your hands on your thigh and bring your back knee to the mat. If you are in Standing Forward Bend, step back with your left leg so your right knee is bent, making sure your knee is aligned over your ankle. Repeat on the other side.

If you have knee pain, place a blanket or fold up the yoga mat underneath your knee.

Benefits:
- Strengthens quadriceps and buttocks
- Opens chest and shoulders (if bringing chest up)
- Strengthens shoulder and wrists (if remaining with hands on ground)
- Stretches hips and abdomen
- Improves balance and concentration

19. Mountain Pose

Mountain Pose with Arms in Fieldgoal Position

Stand with your feet together, big toes touching, heels slightly apart. Try to get all parts of your feet touching the ground (toes and heel). Spread your toes apart if possible. Gently engage your leg muscles, making sure your hips are aligned and not too far forward or back. Lift your chest and gently squeeze your shoulder blades together slightly (like holding an orange between your shoulder blades). Soften your gaze and look straight ahead.

This is known as one of the hardest yoga poses, though it seems simple.

Benefits:

- This is a foundational pose for future balance poses
- Helps with balance
- Provides awareness of your feet connecting with the earth
- Improves posture
- Works on core muscles
- Helps with grounding and improves focus

20. Pigeon Pose

Start in Table Top or Plank Pose. Bend your right knee, bringing it forward so that your right foot is almost touching your left hand, and sit your hips down slowly onto the mat. Keep your foot flexed if your leg is at a 90-degree angle. Make sure the back foot is tucked, pressing into your toes. If you can handle more of a stretch, lean your head forward and bring it down to the mat.

If you have trouble with your knees, then you can angle your bent leg at a 45-degree angle, making sure your toes are pointed.

Make sure your hips are aligned and square, and look over your right shoulder if your right knee is bent. Then come back to center and switch to the other side.

Benefits:

- Opens the hip joints and stretches hip rotators and hip flexors
- Improves posture
- Stretches the spine
- Increases circulation to urinary and digestive systems

21. Plank Pose

There are many ways to get into this pose, and many times this is a transition pose between other poses. You can lie on your stomach and put your hands underneath your shoulders, tuck your toes under and push up. You can also be in Lunge Pose and bring your foot back to Plank Pose. Keep your core muscles firm and buttocks tight. Make sure your wrists are underneath your shoulders and your neck is in a neutral position.

Do not do this pose if you have concerns about your wrist or hands or lower back pain

Alternative is to lower your knees to the mat and lessen the strain on the lower back.

Benefits:
- Core strengthening
- Shoulder stability
- Wrist and hand strength
- Strengthens the back muscles

22. Reclining Butterfly (Bound Angle Pose)

Start in butterfly pose (see #3 above). Exhale, reach your arms back and lower yourself to the floor slowly. You can support your head and neck on a blanket if needed. If your knees do not touch the floor, you can place blocks or blankets underneath them.

If this is too intense of a stretch, then wait until you or the child has more flexibility in the hips to perform this pose.

Benefits:
- Provides a hip-opener pose
- Stimulates internal organs and opens chest and heart
- Helps with digestion
- Stretches inner thigh and groin
- Helps relax lower back
- Relaxes mind and central nervous system

23. Reclined Spinal Twist Pose

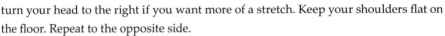

Lie on your back and bring your knees into your chest, then slowly lower your knees to the left side. You can then turn your head to the right if you want more of a stretch. Keep your shoulders flat on the floor. Repeat to the opposite side.

If your knees do not touch the ground in the twist, you can place a blanket underneath your knees.

When bringing your knees to the side, bring them almost to a 45-degree angle with your torso to open up your side body rather than a 90-degree angle that over stretches your lower back.

Benefits:

- Stretches back muscles
- Massages back and hips
- Massages abdominal organs and increases the health of your digestive system
- Encourages movement in your spine and hips
- Stretches piriformis muscle (a muscle in your gluteus region)

24. Rock-n-Roll Pose

Sit on your mat with your back straight and your feet flat on the mat. Grab hold underneath your knees and then roll back and use your momentum to roll back forward again. If you are helping a small child or a child with a physical disability, have them sit in front of you between your legs. Hold them underneath their legs and have them wrap their arms around their shins. Roll back and forth with them in your lap.

Do not do this as an adult with a child if you have back issues or are not strong enough to support the weight of the child.

Benefits:

- Gets the child in an inversion position for a moment, which may be all they can handle if they have vestibular challenges

- Stimulates their nervous system and provides a nice movement for children who are not mobile
- Massages the spine and neck (if child can do it on the mat themselves)
- Increases core strength
- Can be an alerting pose for children

25. Seated Forward Bend

Sit down and stretch both legs straight out in front of you. Have your toes reaching up towards the clouds.
Sit up nice and straight, reach both arms overhead and then slowly lean forward from the hips (not rounding your back). Go just as far as you can. If you cannot reach your toes, that is okay.

Benefits:
- Stretches hamstrings and lower back
- Releases tension in upper body
- Helps calm the brain because your head is lower than your heart
- Increases flexibility of the back and spine

26. Seated Twist Pose

Sit in Easy pose with your back straight. Take a breath in, and as you exhale, turn and look over your right shoulder, reaching your right arm behind you. Make sure your hips stay facing forward. Repeat to the other side.

Some children may only be able to turn their head and eventually be able to turn head, neck and shoulders.

Benefits:
- Opens shoulders and chest
- Increases flexibility in spine
- Strengthens abdominal oblique muscles
- Calms the nervous system (as if "wringing out" your body)

27. Side Angle Twist

Start in Lunge Pose, inhale to stretch up, exhale hands to heart center pressing hands together, inhale and lengthen top of head up (keeping hands at heart center) and exhale to twist. As you hold this pose, with every inhale, lengthen and exhale, and deepen the twist into the pose. Option 2: Put your back knee down

Do not do this pose if you have lower back issues or if the child is unable to maintain her balance.

Benefits:
- Twists the spine, wringing out the abdominal muscles and digestive system
- Increases the flexibility of the spine
- Helps build core strength
- Serves as a balance pose

28. Sleeping Pose

Lie on your back, open your feet about shoulder-width apart and let your feet fall away and relax. Bring your arms down by your side and slightly away from your body with your palms facing up. Relax! Use a blanket or a bolster under your knees if you have back pain, or place a blanket underneath your head. This should be a very relaxed pose.

Benefits:
- Promotes deep relaxation
- Serves as a resting pose
- Promotes focus on your diaphragmatic breathing
- Helps lower blood pressure
- Relieves headache
- Calms the brain and relieves stress

29. Sphinx

Lie on your stomach and bring your hands underneath your shoulders. Bring your head and chest up so you are resting on your forearms. This pose is not as intense as Cobra Pose and can be used as an alternative for children.

Benefits:

- Strengthens the spine
- Opens your chest and lungs, which helps ease breathing and asthma
- Stimulates abdominal organs

30. Standing Forward Bend

Stand in Mountain Pose. As you inhale, reach up high, then as you exhale, bend forward at the hips and reach to the floor. If you cannot touch the floor, just go as far as you can, but make sure you are not bending from your back. You can also bend your knees slightly so you can touch the floor, or you can place your hands on blocks.

Benefits:

- Assumes inversion posture, which is good for the vestibular system (the balance system)
- Calms the brain
- Stimulates liver and kidneys
- Stretches hamstrings and calves
- Reduces fatigue and anxiety

31. Straddle Pose

Sit on the floor, nice and tall, and open the legs into a straddle position. On an inhale, reach up tall with the arms and exhale, bending forward at the hips (not the back), and reach your arms forward. It is fine if you can only go a few inches or if you can reach all the way down, with your stomach touching the floor. Flex your feet.

Do no push a child too far into this pose if they have tight hamstrings

Benefits:
- Stretches inside and back of legs
- Stretches the spine
- Massages abdominal muscles and organs
- Increases blood flow to the pelvis

32. Supported Shoulder Stand Pose

Lie on your back and reach both legs high. Push your hips up, reaching your feet higher up to the ceiling, and place your hands on your back to support yourself. To help facilitate this pose with a child, sit at the child's feet as he is lying on his back. Grab his ankles and slowly lift his legs until he is resting his weight on his shoulders. Then gently lower his legs back down.

Do not do this pose if you have a neck injury, a headache or high blood pressure.

This is an inversion posture and will increase the blood flow to the head and sometimes cause a head rush for children, so watch facial signs in your child to make sure he is comfortable. Also watch the child's energy level; this pose might be fairly alerting, and you may not want to do this before bedtime.

Benefits:
- Stretches neck and spine
- Stimulates thyroid and abdominal organs
- Therapeutic for asthma and helps with lung functioning
- Gets the blood flowing in the opposite direction

33. Tree Pose

Start in Mountain Pose, then bend your right knee, bringing your right foot up and resting it either above or below your knee. Make sure your foot is not resting against your knee. Bring your hands to heart center. Balance there and take several breaths. Once you are stable, you can grow your branches of your tree and reach above your head. When you are ready to come out of the pose, bring your hands to heart center and slowly lower your leg. Repeat on the opposite side.

>   Level one: Hands at heart center
>   Level two: Then reach above head

Benefits:
- Provides a balancing pose and works on core strength
- Improves bilateral coordination
- Improves focus and attention
- Strengthens legs
- Builds self-confidence

34. Triangle Pose

Stand with both feet apart and point your right foot at 90 degrees from your left foot . Align your right heel with the center of your left arch. Squeeze your thighs and stand strong. Inhale, and then as you exhale, reach your body over your right leg and bend from the hips, not the waist. Take your right hand down to your right leg (shin) or to the floor, depending on your flexibility, and reach your left arm up into the air. Turn your head to look up at your left hand. Take slow, deep breaths. Slowly stand up and repeat on the opposite side.

Benefits:
- Strengthens the legs
- Opens the hips
- Reduces stress and anxiety
- Improves digestion

35. Upward Bow Pose

Lie on your back and bend your knees. Bring your heels in as close to your buttocks as possible. Bend your elbows and place your palms on the floor up beside your head with your fingers pointing toward your shoulders. Take a deep breath in and press your body up into the pose, supported by your hands and feet. Take 2-3 deep breaths in this pose and slowly lower yourself back to your mat.

Do not do this pose if you have a headache, back problems or wrist pain. Only perform this pose with a child if you are sure she is flexible and strong enough to hold herself up. If she cannot physically do this, do not facilitate this position, as she could hurt her neck or head.

Benefits:
- Stretches abdominal muscles and chest
- Strengthens back and spine
- Strengthens arms and legs
- Increases energy and alerts the nervous system
- Stimulates the thyroid

36. Warrior 2 Pose

Stand with your hands on your hips and your feet about hip-width apart. Turn your left foot 90 degrees and turn your back to follow, with the right foot turned slightly inward. Make sure your heels are aligned. Bend your left knee, making sure your knee is directly over your ankle. You should distribute your weight evenly between both feet. Then bring your arms out into a T, with the eyes gazing past your left fingers. Perform again on the other side.

Benefits:
- Stretches hips
- Strengthens arms and legs
- Opens chest and lungs
- Improves balance and core strength
- Improves circulation and respiration

Other Great Strengthening Activities You Can Do with Your Child within Your Yoga Sequences:

37. Superman – Prone Extension

Lie on your stomach and reach your arms and legs out long. Take a deep breath in and raise both arms and both legs, trying to get your back into a small arch. If this is too difficult at first, raise only your arms and keep your legs on the ground. Children ages 5-7 should be able to hold this pose for approximately 30 seconds, and children ages 8-10 should be able to hold this for approximately 60 seconds.

Benefits:
- Improves core strength and back extension muscles
- Tests a child's postural control

38. Crunch Hold – Supine Flexion

Lie on your back with your knees bent. Cross your arms across your chest and bring your nose up towards your bent knees. Try to hold this position without holding onto your legs. Children ages 5-7 should be able to hold this pose for approximately 30 seconds, and children ages 8-10 should be able to hold it for approximately 60 seconds.

Benefits:
- Improves core strength
- Promotes head and neck control
- Tests postural control for a child

39. Crab Walking

Sit on the floor and bend your knees. Reach behind you and press your body up on your hands. Try "walking" either forward or backward.

Benefits:
- Strengthens arms, legs, shoulders and ankles
- Strengthens core
- Opens chest and abdominal muscles

40. Bear Walking

Walk forward on your hands with your buttocks in the air

Benefits:
- Strengthens arms, shoulders and wrists
- Increases blood flow through inversion
- Promotes heavy work, which helps regulate the nervous system

41. Frog Hopping

How to get into the Pose: Bend your knees and put your hands on the floor inside the knees. Hop forward like a frog.

Benefits:
- Strengthens legs and arms
- Improves core strength
- Promotes heavy work, which regulates the nervous system, and movement helps with vestibular processing

CHAPTER 5:

YOGA FOR CHILDREN WITH SENSORY CHALLENGES

Creating a Silly Pose

Chapter 5: Yoga for Children with Sensory Challenges

As I discussed earlier, sensory processing refers to the ability to take in information from your environment (and your internal self), process that information affectively in your brain and experience a functional output. We see many children who struggle with sensory processing abilities, and yoga can help them.

Many children with Autism Spectrum Disorder, ADHD, genetic disabilities, Cerebral Palsy (CP), Down Syndrome, developmental delays, etc., ALSO have sensory sensitivities that can affect their daily lives.

If you have a child who is SOR, they might be in fight, flight or freeze mode a lot of the time. These children may exhibit any of the following behaviors:

- Covering their ears when exposed to loud sounds
- Crying when you dress them due to the feel of their clothing or seams in their clothing
- Pulling at the tags in their clothes
- Not enjoying finger painting or touching sticky or gooey things
- Not enjoying eating certain textures or flavors of foods
- Covering their eyes against bright lights
- Expressing fear of swings or being tossed in the air
- Expressing fear of climbing to the top of playground equipment or even feeling scared when their feet are off the ground at all

If a child is sensitive to visual stimuli, then pick a place that does not have much visual stimuli on the walls or in the environment where you are practicing yoga. If your child is visually over-stimulated, it can be hard in the outside environment to decrease the visual stimuli, but you can take action like providing sunglasses when you are outside in the sun and being cautious when taking them to busy places like Costco and theme parks until you know they can handle those situations. The same it applicable for those children are over-responsive to auditory, movement, etc. Ease them into situations you know make them uncomfortable.

For example, if your child screams when you take him to the grocery store and you know it's not just because you said he could not have a cookie, then you may be dealing with a sensory issue, and you need to work up his tolerance to the grocery store. Take him in for just one item and see if he can tolerate buying one thing, checking out and then going back home where he is comfortable. It can also be helpful if the child is old enough to participate in jobs in the store. Have him help find things on the list, a task that can keep him preoccupied.

Sound-cancelling headphones can also help with children who dislike loud sounds or background noises.

If you have a child who exhibits SUR behaviors, she may be slow to respond to stimuli or look as if she is not paying attention to her surroundings. She may:

- Not hear her name being called
- Not feel pain when she is hurt
- Not feel the temperature of water that is too hot until after she has been burned
- Want to go outside in the cold without proper shoes and a jacket
- Look or act lethargic
- Be hard to motivate

Chapter 5: Yoga for Children with Sensory Challenges

If you have a child who is a Sensory Seeker/Craver, he may be very intense and crave certain bodily input constantly. He may:

- Be always on the go
- Give hard hugs and hard high fives
- Be constantly jumping and crashing
- Always want to spin
- Overstuff his mouth
- Talk in a loud voice
- Touch everything or others to the point of annoyance
- Pet animals with too much force

Yoga can benefit all of these children with sensory regulation challenges. Children who are over-responsive can benefit from sequences that use inversion postures.

It is also fun to have children make up some of their own poses, especially if they are nervous, or not ready to sit and follow directions. If you need to get their "buy in" you can have them imitate you, then you imitate them with a pose. After that, you can get them to follow more poses you know will benefit their regulation system.

Yoga Sequence for Children is designed for those who are SOR, have anxiety or seem stressed. These poses help balance both the sympathetic nervous system and parasympathetic nervous system. This sequence will help calm the nervous system and slow down the heart rate and lower blood pressure.

1. Start in Easy Pose (figure 1) with a breathing technique, alternate nostril breathing (see description in Chapter 4) and/or mindful breathing for 3-5 breaths.

2. Perform eye exercises (optional).

figure 1

3. Move into Child's Pose (figure 2); take 5 slow deep breaths.

figure 2

4. Hold Table Top—neutralize spine.

5. Perform Cat/Cow tilts for 5 rounds following a breath (figure 3).

figure 3

6. Step back into Plank Pose (figure 4).

figure 4

7. Hold Downward Dog for 2-3 breaths (figure 5).

figure 5

8. Walk feet up and roll spine slowly up to Mountain Pose (figure 6).

9. Hold Mountain Pose for 2 breaths, bring hands to heart center, inhale, reach arms up and exhale, bringing arms to "field goal" position; this mimics the same breath as Cat/Cow and helps them ground their feet (figure 7).

figure 6

figure 7

10. Breath in, reach up above head, exhale.

11. Hold Chair Pose for 2 breaths (figure 8).

12. Standing Forward, bend, inhale, lift hands to shins and flatten back, then exhale and fold forward to deepen the pose (figure 9).

figure 8

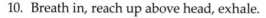

figure 9

13. Lunge right leg back (figure 10).

figure 10

14. Step left foot to meet the right, Plank Pose (figure 11).

figure 11

15. Hold Downward Dog for 2 breaths (adult can press gently on the child's hands to cue them to press into their hands for support). (figure 12).

figure 12

16. Step feet up, inhale, and stand up to Mountain Pose (repeat) (figure 13).

figure 13

17. Standing Forward Bend (figure 14).

figure 14

18. Lunge left leg back (figure 15).

figure 15

19. Step right leg back to meet the left Plank Pose (figure 16).

figure 16

20. Hold Downward Dog for 2 breaths (figure 17).

figure 17

21. Bring toes together and lower into Child's Pose, hold for 2 breaths—in Child's Pose, if a child wants, she can bring her arms down by her side and grab the heels of her feet (figure 18).

figure 18

22. Slowly rise to a seated position, with hands at heart center. Straighten both legs out straight, reach arms up, inhale.

23. On the exhale, Seated Forward Bend and hold for 2-3 breaths, both legs out. Slowly sit back up (figure 19).

figure 19

24. Inhale reach arms up, exhale Head to Knee Forward Bend Pose right leg out and then left leg out (figure 20).

figure 20

25. Straddle Forward Bend (figure 21).

figure 21

26. Seated Twist to both sides (figure 22).

figure 22

27. Lie on your back for Happy Baby Pose (figure 23).

figure 23

28. Assume the Sleeping Pose for relaxation (figure 24).

figure 24

Children who are under-responsive need input to their bodies to help them alert. The following sequences can be helpful for those children. There could be many variations of this sequence, but these poses will help to alert and wake your child up so she is ready to learn and take on the world!

Alerting sequence—

1. Easy Pose—3 slow deep breaths (figure 1).

figure 1

2. Bellows Breath (alerting their nervous system).

3. Eye exercises (optional).

4. Table Top Pose.

5. Cat/Cow for 5 rounds of breaths (figure 2).

figure 2

6. Cross your feet behind you and sit back into Easy Pose (figure 3).

figure 3

7. Seated twist both sides, holding for 3-4 breaths on each side (figure 4).

figure 4

8. Come down onto your stomach.

9. Take a deep breath in and press up into Cobra or Sphinx Pose, depending on flexibility (figure 5).

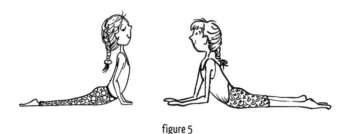

figure 5

10. Release back down to your mat, bend your knees in and reach back to grab your feet.

11. Bow Pose or Alternate Bow for younger or less flexible kids. Hold for 3-4 breaths (figure 6).

12. Relax back down onto your mat, bringing your arms forward, getting ready to be a snake again. Press up into Cobra or Sphinx, hold 3-4 breaths (figure 7).

figure 6

figure 7

13. Downward Dog hold for 2-3 breaths (figure 8).

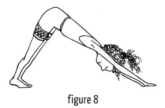

figure 8

14. Lunge Pose right leg first, bring your torso up and stretch hip (hold for 3-4 breaths) (figure 9).

figure 9

15. Step up into Standing Forward Bend (figure 10).

figures 10

figure 11

16. Reach up into Mountain and reach arms overhead, stretching on an inhale, then exhale and (figure 11).

17. Standing Forward Bend (figure 12).

figures 12

18. Step back with right leg so you are in left Lunge, bring torso up to stretch hip (hold for 3-4 breaths) (figure 13).

figure 13

19. Step up to top of mat stand in Mountain Pose for 2-3 breaths (figure 14).

figure 14

20. Tree Pose both sides (figure 15).

figure 15

21. Rock-n-Roll 3-4 times (figure 16).

figure 16

22. Supported Shoulder Stand; make sure you are breathing (figure 17).

figure 17

23. Bridge Pose (figure 18).

figure 18

24. Upward Bow or Fish Pose, depending on child's age and level (figure 19).

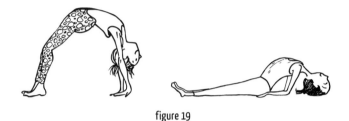

figure 19

25. You can repeat this whole sequence starting from Cat/Cow, or you can move into

26. Reclined Spinal Twist; hold for 3-4 breaths on each side (figure 20).

figure 20

27. Sleeping Pose for relaxation. If you have time, stay here for 10 minutes (figure 21).

figure 21

For those students who are more of a sensory seeker or craver type of child, they may be constantly looking for input and need intense heavy work activities to help with regulation. The following sequences will be helpful for these children.

1. Start in Mountain Pose, take 3 slow deep breaths (figure 1).

figure 1

2. Standing Forward Bend, with hands on the mat and step feet back (figure 2).

figure 2

3. Plank Pose (figure 3).

figure 3

4. Press up into Downward Dog, step right foot up to meet hands (figure 4).

figure 4

5. Warrior 2 right side (figure 5).

figure 5

6. Side Angle Twist (figure 6).

figure 6

7.   Triangle Pose right side then step feet together (figure 7).

figure 7

8.   Mountain Pose, inhale reach arms overhead, exhale (figure 8).

figure 8

9.   Standing Forward Bend, hands on the mat and step back to (figure 9).

figure 9

10. Plank Pose (figure 10).

11. Downward Dog, step let foot up to
    meet hands (figure 11).

figure 10

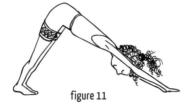

figure 11

12. Warrior 2 left side (figure 12).

figure 12

13. Side Angle Twist (figure 13).

figure 13

14. Triangle Pose left side, then step feet together (figure 14).

figure 14

15. Mountain Pose inhale reach arms up, as you exhale, bend forward (figure 15).

figure 15

16. Standing Forward Bend, hands on the mat and step feet back (figure 16).

figure 16

17. Plank Pose (figure 17).

figure 17

18. Bring right knee in front at 90 degree angle or 45 degree angle (read description); Pigeon Pose right side (figure 18).

figure 18

19. Bring right leg back to meet the left, Plank Pose (figure 19).

20. Lower into Cobra or Sphinx (figure 20).

figure 19

figure 20

21. Downward Dog (figure 21).

figure 21

22. Plank Pose (figure 22).

23. Bring left knee in front (read description) Pigeon Pose Left side (figure 23).

figure 22

figure 23

24. Bring left leg back to meet the right; Plank Pose lower into Cobra or Sphinx (figure 24).

25. Table top, neutral spine.

figure 24

26. Cat/Cow 3 rounds with breath slowly (figure 25).

figure 25

27. Child's Pose hold for 3-4 breaths (figure 26).

figure 26

28. Butterfly Pose stretch and hold 4-5 breaths (figure 27).

figure 27

29. Seated Forward Bend—both legs out straight (figure 28).

figure 28

30. Straddle Pose (figure 29).

figure 29

31. Seated Twists both sides (figure 30).

figure 30

32. Mindful Breathing 3-5 breaths and/or breath in for 3 counts and out for 5 counts.

33. Eye Exercises (optional).

34. Lie down on your back.

35. Bridge Pose (figure 31).

figure 31

36. Knee to Chest Pose right leg, then left leg (figure 32).

figure 32

37. Reclined Butterfly (Bound Angle Pose); hold for 5 breaths (figure 33).

figure 33

38. Sleeping Pose—stay here for 10 mins, if possible (figure 34).

figure 34

Now WAIT, you may say. *My kid is over-responsive to auditory, is under-responsive to tactile input and craves vestibular and proprioceptive input! What do I do for my child?*

You can try various sequences and mix up the poses a little to see what will work best for your child. One day the calming sequence might be better, and another day the alerting sequence might be better. You will also learn as you practice yoga yourself more and your child practices that you can find other new poses to challenge them that will help with emotion regulation and cognitive skills. As children get older, they can handle more complex poses. Work with your yoga instructor to figure out what those poses might be for you and your child.

Calming sequence—short activities to help when you may not have time to do a full 20-30 minute session with your child.

- Perform deep breathing—Experts say that taking 3 slow deep breaths helps reset the brain and send neuropathways of calming serotonin down into the blood stream and helps expand the lungs, which helps calm your nervous system down. According to the research being done on mindfulness, taking 3-5 slow deep breaths is also calming, as it helps the amygdala (emotional) part of your brain "reset."

- Decrease stimuli in the environment—Turn down the lights, use low, soft floor lamps when possible, either eliminate external noise, or use calming music that can be helpful and lower your voice when interacting with a child who seems overwhelmed.

- Give slow, deep pressure to the body if your child is craving proprioceptive input. Postures that can be good for this are Downward Dog, Child's Pose, Triangle Pose, Plank Pose, Mountain Pose and Tree Pose.

- You can mix up some of the yoga sequences to make them work for your child as long as you are moving safely and slowly though the poses and watching your child's reactions to make sure you are getting the effect you are looking for.

- For example, if you think your child needs to calm down and you have them do jumping jacks but you see that this activity revs him up, you know that you need to choose a different activity for your child in that moment.

Postural Disorder and Praxis (Motor Planning)

Many children with SPD and other disabilities also have trouble with core strength, maintaining upright postural control and developing motor planning skills.

Some children have lower muscle tone (for example, children with Down Syndrome) and need to work on their overall muscle strength to help with simple things like crawling, walking, balancing on one foot and putting their pants on, or jumping with two feet. Yoga can help not only strengthen the muscles but also help with bilateral coordination. Yoga is a great tool to help build strength, stretch the muscles and help improve core strength and balance skills. Almost all children and adults can benefit from yoga for these reasons alone.

Remember, praxis is the ability to generate an idea, sequence a task and then motor plan (execute) that task; for example, crawling across the room, getting dressed or making a birthday card for Mom or Dad. Some children struggle with some or all of the parts of praxis, and yoga can help build these skills.

If you are practicing yoga with a child, he will be required to either imitate you or follow your directions or your physical guidance. This will help him sequence and motor plan. Once you have advanced his skills and he is safe in the poses and routine, then you can sequence together several poses and have the child follow these. Then he can sequence himself through a few. This takes good coordination and motor planning skills, and since the challenge can be highly motivating to the child (vs. making them brush their teeth), you may see improvement in other areas of the child's daily life. He may sequence the task of washing his hands. He may follow multiple-step directions better. He may also show improved motor planning to physically execute difficult tasks such as tying his shoes, doing jumping jacks and riding a bike, because you have been working on his focus, strength, flexibility, breathing, control and balance. You can also use a visual schedule to help children know which poses will come next. This can help those children who struggle initially with motor planning and then slowly fade those visual prompts.

For children who struggle with either of these two sensory subtypes, all the yoga sequences will help them gain core strength, balance and bilateral coordination. There are poses that specifically focus on that more so than others.

Yoga Poses that focus on core strength:

- Bridge Pose
- Bow Pose
- Cobra Pose
- Crescent Moon Pose
- Extended Cat Pose
- Lunge Pose
- Mountain Pose
- Pigeon Pose
- Plank Pose
- Rock-n-Roll Pose
- Seated Twist Pose
- Sphinx Pose
- Supported Shoulder Stand
- Tree Pose
- Triangle Pose
- Upward Bow Pose
- Warrior 2 Pose

Yoga Poses that help improve balance and bilateral coordination:

- Bow Pose
- Crescent Moon Pose
- Downward Dog Pose
- Extended Cat Pose
- Lunge Pose
- Mountain Pose
- Plank Pose
- Rock-n-Roll Pose
- Seated Spinal Twist
- Standing Forward Bend
- Supported Shoulder Stand
- Tree Pose
- Triangle Pose
- Upward Bow Pose
- Warrior 2 Pose

Interview with Allison Merlo

Allison Merlo, M.S. OTR/L RYT, was born and raised on Long Island, New York. She graduated from the University of Scranton in Scranton, Pennsylvania, with her masters in Occupational Therapy. Allison is now living in Arizona, working as a pediatric occupational therapist full time in a school district in South Phoenix and is also working part time in a pediatric clinic in Central Phoenix. Allison is very passionate about traveling to underdeveloped countries and has experience working with children in orphanages, rehabilitation centers as well as homes in Mexico City, Guyana, Haiti and Costa Rica. Allison is a co-founder of Outreach Theraplay, Inc., an organization that funds therapy and play equipment for children in underdeveloped areas of the world. She simultaneously works domestically in the United States to educate and train local businesses and families of children with special needs on appropriate modifications for social engagement. Allison has experience and training in Brain Gym Educational Kinesiology, Handwriting without Tears, Advanced Brain Technologies, The Listening Program and Yoga for the Special Child. Allison also completed her 200-hour yoga teacher training and is a registered yoga instructor. Allison uses yoga as a sensory motor "warm-up" activity and a self-regulatory exercise for children with sensory needs. In her free time, Allison enjoys running, swimming, biking, surfing, hiking and just being out in nature! She runs marathons, is a USA triathlon member and loves to practice yoga!

Chapter 5: Yoga for Children with Sensory Challenges

What has your yoga training been like in Costa Rica?

This training is amazing! It is very intense and comprehensive, as one would expect for 21 days to complete 200-hour teacher training certification. It is a lot of memorization of alignment for all poses, sequencing, Sanskrit translations and yoga philosophy encompassed in a holistic manner through values taught, meditation, lifestyle, etc.

How do you see OT and yoga going hand in hand?

In knowing, studying and practicing occupational therapy with both adults and children in skilled nursing facilities, hand clinics, schools, home health and outpatient clinics, I have come to realize that the most important aspect of this profession is the connection or union and the rapport you form with your client. Ultimately, the goal of our profession as occupational therapists is to be a catalyst, motivator and educator for our clients to fulfill their life goals, whatever they may be. Yoga and OT can go hand in hand to improve so many areas of our lives. For example, in an acute setting, that may be the ability to perform dressing tasks with less assistance; in a school it may be to produce legible handwriting; in a clinic it may be to increase hand strength and mobility to return to playing the guitar after a crush injury or in a pediatric clinic it may teach a child to initiate play with peers. Whatever it may be, occupational therapists are there to make it happen, despite the impeding condition. In essence, this involves a keen awareness of sensory issues. Sensations are everywhere, in what we hear, see, feel, do, etc. It is ultimately our interpretation of the world. We all have sensory sensitivities, and we all have different thresholds, meaning we all tolerate a varying amount of sensory stimulation or experience. Some of us may get startled at loud noises; some of us may experience headaches with bright lights. It is our responsibility as occupational therapists to be sensitive to our clients' sensory needs and gain sensory awareness. This involves a great deal of individualized instruction and attention with a keen presence and awareness of the individual and their unique capabilities. With both mental and physical presence, we can do amazing, transformational things. It is our first responsibility as occupational therapists to be present. Therefore, occupational therapists cultivate a union with their clients with a keen sensory awareness and presence.

As Britt has explained to you, yoga comes from the Sanskrit root *yuj*, which means to join, unite or to yoke through a harmonizing system of development for the body, mind and spirit. As I stated above, an occupational therapist, whether working with children or adults, needs to first establish a connection or union with each individual client. Within this union, transformation takes place. The ultimate aim or goal of yoga is one of self-development and self-realization. This too is the aim of occupational therapy. To reach occupational therapy goals, whether big or small, and experience self-development, self-realization should be cultivated.

Yoga asanas, or poses, are physical poses and therefore can make up a sensory motor exercise. Children today are expected to sit for long periods of time in classrooms and education settings. Children are denied the utmost need to move, control their own bodies, expend energy and take a deep breath and relax! A keen sensory awareness of what each child or client needs is necessary to reach goals both in therapy and out in the community. Yoga teaches children to focus on their breath and learn about their bodies by moving and exploring! This ultimately allows children to calm down, attend and focus to meet the demands of today's education system. As occupational therapists, yoga can be used to facilitate a child's optimal functioning based on sensory needs.

Lastly, yoga itself encompasses more than the poses you may see people doing on their yoga mats. Yoga begins with presence. Breathing and meditation is a large component of yoga, and this requires one to be fully present and aware. As occupational therapists, we need to be present to best serve our clients. It is also important for us to teach our clients to be present themselves. This can start with simply breathing, sitting and being. Once this is established, transformation can and will take place.

What types of children do you mostly work with? And how do you see yoga benefiting those children?

I am a full-time school occupational therapist in a Title One school district in southwest Phoenix, Arizona. I am at six different schools within this school district. I work with children who have individualized education plans (IEP) ranging from preschool through eighth grade. These children are receiving occupational therapy based on their IEPs due to their specific academic needs. I also work part time at a pediatric outpatient clinic that provides physical, occupational, music and speech therapies for children from birth to 21 years. Some of the conditions I see on a daily basis in both the school district and the clinic are autism spectrum disorder, attention deficit disorder, hydrocephalus, developmental delay, intellectual delay, cerebral palsy, seizure disorder and Rett's syndrome, among others.

I practice yoga as a sensory motor warm-up activity for most of my school-age children. It is an activity they enjoy, they love to imitate the poses, and they have fun! I like to grade it by increasing the difficulty or sequencing the poses, depending on the child. Overall, I have seen yoga to help my children with developmental delays, noting an increase in openness and communication. It also assists with muscle tone and body spatial awareness, as I have seen children integrate fluidity in their movements and coordination on and off the mat. For some of my clients who lack physical ability to move in ways yoga requires, breathing techniques, relaxation techniques and yoga-inspired range of motion has proved effective.

What advice do you have for other therapists wanting to use yoga as a tool to add to their current practice with children with special needs?

My advice to other practitioners is to first establish their own practice of yoga. With a personal practice, yoga can manifest a practitioner into the best catalyst for change for their clients. It is with this that a keen awareness, presence and union provide an opportunity to best treat each individual. Incorporating yoga into therapy can begin with breathing techniques and graduate up to poses and eventually sequences. This makes for increased complexity and grading of therapeutic activity physically, cognitively and spiritually. It is important to have this holistic connection as occupational therapists, because we are dealing with each individual's unique life situation, and that requires our utmost presence to embody the role as a catalyst, motivator and educator.

CHAPTER 6:

YOGA FOR CHILDREN WITH AUTISM SPECTRUM DISORDER

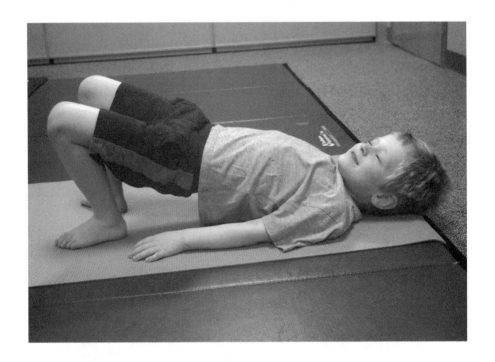

Bridge Pose

hat is Autism Spectrum Disorder (ASD)?

ASD is defined in the *DSM-V* (Diagnostic Statistical Manual 5th edition) as:

A. Persistent deficits in social communication and social interaction across contexts, not accounted for by general developmental delays, and manifest by all three of the following:

- Deficits in social emotional reciprocity; ranging from abnormal social approach and failure of normal back and forth conversation through reduced sharing of interests, emotions and affect and response of total lack of initiation of social interaction
- Deficits in nonverbal communicative behaviors used for social interaction
- Deficits in developing and maintaining relationships

B. Restrictive repetitive patterns of behavior, interests or activities as manifested by at least two of the following:

- Stereotyped or repetitive speech, motor movements, or use of objects
- Excessive adherence to routines, ritualized patterns of verbal or nonverbal behavior, or excessive resistance to change
- Highly restricted, fixated interests that are abnormal in intensity or focus
- Hyper- or hypo-reactivity to sensory input or unusual interest in sensory aspects of environment (such as apparent indifference to

pain/heat/cold, adverse response to specific sounds or textures, excessive smelling or touching of objects, fascination with lights or spinning objects).

C. Symptoms must be present in early childhood (but may not become fully manifested until social demands exceed limited capacities)

D. Symptoms together limit and impair everyday functioning

The term Asperger syndrome is no longer in use, according to the *DSM-V*, but I still feel that many people who are "Aspies" relate to that terminology more so than having autism. I think there are other children who are smart, quirky, may have delayed social skills, and seem to have that interesting way about looking at life that makes me feel they relate more to Asperger syndrome. Many children identify themselves as having "high functioning autism," and that is great too. Foremost, you are a person, and it does not matter what your diagnosis is; it's how you function in your day-to-day life that helps me determine what your strengths and challenges are and how to proceed going forward with therapy tools and strategies to help.

There are many children on the ASD spectrum who are non-verbal or have low language skills. Others may have language but are very rigid in their thinking or routines. Sometimes it's nice to have the child choose 3 poses and then you as the adult choose three poses if you have a child who is very rigid in his or her thinking and behavior. It is also a great idea to use visuals with children on the autism spectrum, especially if they are familiar with this in other areas of their school and home life. You can have pictures of poses with the names and make sure you change up the order after a few times to prevent children from getting stuck into the same routine. We want to gradually help children learn to be flexible. This is also a skill that needs to be taught in many other areas of their day, not just during yoga practice. Yoga provides multi-level learning for students with disabilities. This makes it great for children who are visual learners, especially for students with ASD. It is good for teachers/instructors to position themselves at the students' eye level, using their body as a visual tool to help these children learn (Goldberg, 2004).

No matter where your child may fall on the autism spectrum, they all can benefit from yoga therapy.

Possible signs of autism:

- Lining up toys
- Inability to tolerate someone else playing with their toys or changing what they are doing (difficulty transitioning)
- Decreased eye contact
- Decreased language skills, difficulty communicating (little or no verbal skills)
- Constantly repeating words or short groups of words, memorizing and repeating entire TV shows
- Crying fits and tantrums for no reason
- Display of little or no emotional connection with others
- Inability to pretend play
- Repeated body movements (stimming, such as hand or arm flapping, rocking, and hitting themselves over and over again.)
- Fear of people (at parks, family functions, in public and at home)
- Lack of fear (unaware of any safety concerns or danger)
- Overt fascination and obsession with one item or subject for an extended period

How to Deal with Behavior Issues

What do you do if your child or a child you are working with refuses to take part in or come to the yoga mat to even start? One suggestion is to make the room nice and calm, with low lights and calming music. Have no other distractions in the room or things for the child to get into. Then sit on your mat and move slowly through some poses, or sit and chant. Many times that child will eventually come to the mat or watch you from a distance and then realize that the demands you are placing are small and that you are not going to force him to do anything. This may take a few sessions for success. If you think a visual schedule will help, try that. If you think even just getting that child to sit cross-legged and clap with you or even just take a few breaths is enough for the day, great; move on and try again the next time.

I have had children take a few weeks to finally get to where they are ready to imitate the poses I am showing them. Then if I have a good relationship with them, I can help physically guide them through some poses. If they dislike being touched (like we discussed in Chapter 5) slow down and let them imitate you. If you feel they are not moving into and out of the poses safely, then try an easier pose so they are not compromising their body posture.

We know that almost all children who are on the autism spectrum also have sensory processing challenges. That being said, you can look at the different subtypes of sensory modulation and decide how to choose a sequence that will help your child with autism. Is she a child who seeks input to her nervous system and needs more grounding heavy work type of yoga and activities, or is she more anxious and in fight or flight mode and in need of more calming soothing yoga poses and activities?

Chapter 6: Yoga for Children with Autism Spectrum Disorder

If your child or a child you are working with has limited communication, has limited focus and attention and needs to start small, here are ideas for those types of kiddos.

Anxiety in Kids

Many children with anxiety look a lot like our SOR kiddos. The same sequences we used for calming there can be used for children with anxiety. Make sure you are teaching them the various breathing techniques and teaching them how to use their breath to get through an "anxious" experience. Using mindfulness is going to help these types of kiddos with overall sensory regulation. Please see Chapter 12 for more details about Mindful Life™.

Interview with Amber Waheed, PhD

Dr. Amber Waheed has been working as a school psychologist for the past fifteen years, intervening with students ranging in ages from 3 to 21 and spending time in schools and residential treatment centers. She conducts assessments and provides intervention strategies for students with social emotional challenges as well as learning disabilities. She recently obtained her doctorate from the University of Denver, with a focus on assessing the perceptions of giftedness for parents of culturally and linguistically diverse families. Prior to her doctorate, Dr. Waheed obtained an Education Specialist degree from the University of Colorado with a focus on intervention strategies with students. She currently resides in Centennial, Colorado with her husband and two children.

What are your thoughts on how yoga can help children with anxiety?

The increase in anxiety disorders observed in schools is hindering children's ability to maximize their learning potential and develop positive peer relationships. Anxiety, an umbrella term used to include such conditions as Social Anxiety Disorder, Post-Traumatic Stress Disorder, School Phobia, and Separation Anxiety, interferes with a child's ability to manage and cope with the academic, social and psychological demands of everyday life. Given the research centered on yoga with children, we know that yoga is a healthy alternative approach to help intervene with children who suffer from anxiety. Encouraging children to develop positive stress management techniques will allow them greater ability to cope with the stressors of everyday life, maximize their ability to learn and develop positive pro-social relationships with others.

Research shows slow, deep breaths can help calm the body. How does this work?

Slow breathing during yoga is intended to reduce the heart rate, respiratory rate and blood pressure, which are direct responses to the anxious state (Telles et al., 2009). Practitioners can practice various breathing techniques with children to help children get a sense of calm. Belly breaths, volcano breaths, and bumblebee breaths are all effective ways to encourage breathing amongst students. (Please refer to Chapter 4, where Britt describes in more detail the various types of breathing.)

Chapter 6: Yoga for Children with Autism Spectrum Disorder

Explain the benefits of yoga on the brain and other systems of the body.

The latest research on brain development is exciting, as we discover how exposure to different stimuli can change neural pathways and change levels of neurotransmitters in the brain. For instance, low levels of Y-aminobutyric acid (GABA) found in the brain leads to an increase of mood and anxiety disorders. Researchers have found that a significant increase of GABA levels was observed in participants who completed a 60-minute yoga session (Steeter et al., 2010). We also know that yoga movements increase blood and oxygen levels throughout the body and positively affect both the central and autonomic nervous systems, which are crucial in helping us calm our bodies in highly aroused or anxious states (Peck et al., 2005).

One of the more significant discoveries explored at Harvard University involves changes to the brain after eight weeks of yoga (Lazar, 2014). This includes areas of the left hippocampus (associated with learning, cognitive, memory and emotional regulation), the amygdala (associated with managing anxiety, fear and stress), temporal parietal junction (associated with perspective taking, empathy and compassion) and gray matter (associated with working memory and executive functioning skills). Yoga helps improve the functioning of the mind, which allows for students' greater ability to deal with stressful or anxiety-provoking situations.

What are other techniques to help children with anxiety?

Various treatment and intervention strategies are effective with students showing anxiety symptoms. Depending on the level of maladjustment of the anxiety disorder and the impact on the child's daily functioning, various treatments are encouraged. Therapy, including cognitive behavioral therapy (CBT) and dialectical behavioral therapy (DBT), are most commonly used when treating students with anxiety disorders. However, under more severe circumstances, medications known as serotonin reuptake inhibitors (SSRIs) can be described by a psychiatrist. However, it is important to note that serious side effects may emerge as a result of the use of these medications. This includes interference with one's cognitive abilities and emotional dysregulation. In some instances, suicidal ideation may develop. Frequent and consistent check-ups with the prescribing doctor are encouraged to monitor the impact of the medications.

Other non-traditional forms of therapy may include art therapy and deep-pressure therapy. Art therapy involves allowing students to make art to gain a sense of calm without the stress of verbally communicating with the therapist/practitioner. It allows children to focus on the moment, distracting them from anxiety-provoking thoughts. Deep pressure, also a non-verbal activity, encourages the practitioner or parent to apply gentle but firm pressure to the body of an anxious person with a pressure garment or other method (i.e., deep-pressure vest, weighted lap pad, etc.). This is often facilitated by an occupational therapist to determine what type of pressure will benefit the student and should be determined prior to when a student is in anxious or in an aroused state.

Short Yoga Sequence Using a Visual Schedule

Make sure you have visuals to show your child and keep it consistent for a few sessions, and then, as their tolerance permits, slowly change up a few poses, change an order of a pose or change how you get into and out of the pose safely.

- Child's Pose (grounding/calming/easy) – practice breathing here (figure 1)

figure 1

- Butterfly Pose – make this active and fun, pretend you are flying somewhere, gently flapping your knees as your "wings" (figure 2)

figure 2

figure 3

- Lion Pose – allow the children to use their voice in any sound (figure 3)
- Table Top – then Cat/Cow tilt (figure 4)

figure 4

figure 5

- Mountain Pose – reach high, inhale, and on the exhale, fold over from the hips (figure 5)

- Standing Forward Bend – hold for 2-3 breaths (figure 6)

figure 6

- Mountain Pose – can bring hands to heart center and press hands together (figure 7)

figure 7

- Crescent Moon Pose – both sides (figure 8)
- Rock-n-Roll (figure 9)

figure 8

figure 9

- Happy Baby Pose (figure 10)

figure 10

- Knee to Chest Right then Left – many children with autism have digestive issues, and this can help (figure 11)

figure 11

- Sleeping Pose – Try to get the child to hold even for 5 minutes if possible, but if they can only tolerate 2 minutes, start there and increase each time you practice with them. (figure 12)

figure 12

Pose Sequence to Help You and Your Child Sleep Better

- Start with 5 mindful breaths
- Easy Pose or Kneeling for alternate nostril breathing (figure 1)
- Seated Forward Bend (figure 2)

figure 1

figure 2

- Head to Knee Forward Bend – right, then left leg (figure 3)

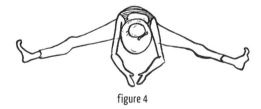

figure 3

- Straddle Pose (figure 4)

figure 4

- Seated Twist – both sides (figure 5)

figure 5

- Child's Pose (figure 6)

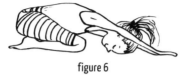

figure 6

- Legs up the Wall with pillow under lower back – you can put a weighted animal on the top of their feet (figure 7)

figure 7

- Reclined Butterfly Pose (Bound Angle Pose) – place pillow underneath stops at lumbar spine (figure 8)

figure 8

- You can also place your child in this position in his bed or on the floor to help him sleep. Place him on his stomach over pillow with arms in field goal position; hips need to be at edge of the pillow and knees bent to the side. Try both sides if your child is a tummy sleeper

- You can also try Child's Pose over their pillow on their stomach. *You can place a weighted animal on their back, chest, hips, or wherever they like more sensory input.*
- Sleeping Pose – place the pillow underneath their back and edge of pillow stop at the lumbar spine so the bottom is on the floor (figure 9)

figure 9

- Deep breathing – have her practice diaphragmatic breathing to relax herself here.

If your child has trouble with digestion, please see the yoga sequence for better digestion in Chapter 8.

CHAPTER 7:

YOGA FOR CHILDREN WITH ADD/ADHD

Tree Pose

hat is ADD/ADHD?

According to the Mayo Clinic, "Attention-deficit/hyperactivity disorder (ADHD) is a chronic condition that affects millions of children and often persists into adulthood. ADHD includes a combination of problems, such as difficulty sustaining attention, hyperactivity and impulsive behavior. Attention-deficit/hyperactivity disorder (ADHD) has been called attention-deficit disorder (ADD) in the past. But ADHD is now the preferred term because it describes both of the primary features of this condition: inattention and hyperactive-impulsive behavior.[8]

Even though you may notice some signs and symptoms of what looks like ADD in a young child (3 to 4 years old), usually it is not diagnosed until after the age of 5. Most children under the age of 5 have a short attention span because they are exploring and learning, and that is typical development. My personal recommendations regarding children with ADD/ADHD are thus: if you feel it is affecting the child's learning at home or at school, try therapy first. Try occupational therapy, cognitive therapy, learning support or yoga therapy to see if you can help provide helpful coping strategies before trying medication. I believe that medication definitely has its place, and sometimes it is needed to help a child, but I like to suggest that families try alternatives first before moving to a medication for their child.

Signs and symptoms of ADHD may include:

- Difficulty paying attention
- Easily distracted
- Difficulty following through on instructions
- Frequent problems organizing tasks or activities
- Fidgeting or having a hard time sitting in their seat in the classroom
- Daydreaming
- Losing items frequently
- Failure to finish schoolwork/homework, chores or other tasks
- Difficulty remaining seated and seeming to be in constant motion
- Appears to not be listening
- Excessive talking and inability to stop and listen to what others have to say. Sometimes finishing others' sentences for them
- Frequently interrupts or intrudes on others' conversations or games
- Frequently has trouble waiting for his/her turn

How Can Yoga Benefit Children with ADD/ADHD?

Roxanne Naseem Rashedi comments, "Breathing techniques can greatly benefit children with ADHD. Similar to practicing asanas, breathing techniques work to neutralize the SNS and PNS and connect more communication between the right and left hemispheres of the brain—a difficulty for some children with special needs."

Children with ADD/ADHD can benefit from yoga because it teaches focus and discipline. You can make it fun or serious for a child, depending on their age and current abilities. You can start with 15 to 20 minutes of yoga and then increase the duration as the child can become more focused on the task at hand.

Sequences Used for ADHD

The following sequences are best to help improve attention. This works for children who are also sensory seekers (see Chapter 5 for more on sensory seekers) and/or have ADD/ADHD.

1. Start with 3 to 5 mindful breaths in a seated position. Being aware of your breath, relax the shoulders and feel the breath into your belly.
2. Alternate nostril breathing.
3. Table Top Pose.
4. Cat/Cow Pose for 3 rounds of breath (figure 1).

figure 1

5. Extended Cat Pose – hold both sides for 2 to 3 breaths (figure 2).

figure 2

6. Child's Pose – hold for 2 breaths (figure 3).

figure 3

7. Mountain Pose – hold for 3 to 4 breaths. Inhale and reach up with both arms. As you exhale, fold forward from the hips, keeping your back flat (figure 4).

8. Standing Forward Bend – hold for 2 to 3 breaths. Step your left leg back to prepare for Right Lunge (figure 5).

figure 4

figures 5

9. Right Lunge – bring chest up and knee to the floor for 2 breaths (figure 6).

figure 6

10. Plank Pose – lower yourself to the floor and prepare for cobra (figure 7).

figure 7

11. Cobra Pose – hold for 2 to 3 breaths, then lift hips up, moving into (figure 8).

12. Downward Dog – hold for 2-3 breaths, bring left knee forward (figure 9).

figure 8

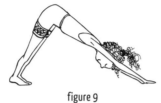

figure 9

13. Left Lunge – bring chest up and knee to the floor for 2 breaths (figure 10).

figure 10

14. Plank Pose (figure 11).

figure 11

15. Cobra Pose – hold for 2 to 3 breaths, then lift hips up into (figure 12).

figure 12

16. Downward Dog – hold for 2-3 breaths, walk feet up to the top of your mat and slowly roll yourself up one vertebra at a time (figure 13).

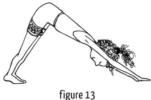

figure 13

17. Mountain Pose – reach arms up as you inhale, then exhale and fold forward from the hips (figure 14).
18. Standing Forward Bend – hold for 2 breaths (figure 15).

figure 14

figures 15

19. Tree Pose – right foot bent in (figure 16).

figure 16

20. Mountain Pose (figure 17).
21. Crescent Moon – inhale arms up, lean to the right, back to neutral and then to the left (figure 18).

figure 17

figure 18

22. Tree Pose – left food bent in (figure 19).
23. Chair Pose – hold for 2 to 3 breaths (figure 20).

figure 19

figure 20

24. Mountain Pose – to prepare for next pose, step your right foot back, keeping your left foot facing the front, bending the left knee (figure 21).

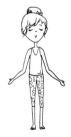

figure 21

25. Warrior 2 – straighten back leg arms out into a T, inhale, reach to front of mat and exhale (figure 22).

figure 22

26. Side Angle Twist (figure 23).

figure 23

27. Triangle Pose – straighten both legs in Triangle with arms in a T, inhale lean towards your front leg and then reach down to your shin, block or ankle, depending on flexibility (figure 24).

figure 24

28. Step back up to the top of your mat, then step back with your left foot, keeping your right foot facing the front, bending the right knee.

29. Warrior 2 – straighten back leg arms out in a T, inhale, reach to front of mat and exhale (figure 25).

figure 25

30. Side Angle Twist (figure 26).

figure 26

31. Triangle Pose – straighten both legs into Triangle with arms in a T, inhale, lean towards your front leg and then reach down to your shin, block or ankle, depending on flexibility (figure 27).

figure 27

32. Mountain Pose – hands at heart center, sit down on the floor (figure 28).

33. Seated Forward Bend – both legs straight out (figure 29).

figure 28

figure 29

34. Seated Spinal Twist – both sides (figure 30).

35. Supported Shoulder Stand – use blankets or a pillow for support (figure 31).

figure 30

figure 31

36. Fish Pose (figure 32).

37. Seated Meditation or Sleeping Pose for deep Relaxation – try to encourage child to be calm for 5 to 10 minutes, even longer if possible (figure 33).

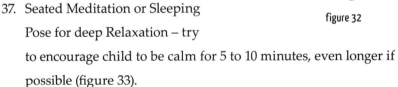

figure 32

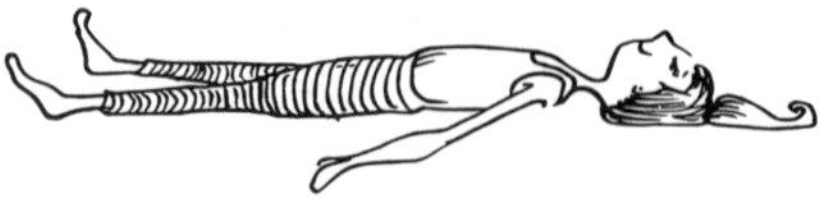

figure 33

You can go back through this sequence a little faster if the child understands the body movement, so instead of holding the poses, move through them like a Flow type of yoga sequence.

CHAPTER 8:

YOGA FOR CHILDREN WHO ARE MEDICALLY FRAGILE AND/OR WITH PHYSICAL CHALLENGES

Happy Baby Pose

Chapter 8: Yoga for Children Who Are Medically Fragile and/or with Physical Challenges

Cerebral Palsy and Other Motor Delays

According to the National Institute of Neurological Disorders and Stroke, Cerebral Palsy (CP) is any of the neurological disorders that occur in pregnancy, infancy or early childhood. This disorder typically affects children's physical body and muscle coordination and sometimes their cognitive ability. CP has a wide spectrum of challenges that can affect a child, from mild to severe. CP is caused by an abnormality in the brain that controls muscle movements, and it can also be caused by a childhood illness such as meningitis, a head injury or accident. There are many benefits of yoga for children with any level of CP.

There are other muscular disorders that affect motor coordination that could include Muscular Dystrophy, Down syndrome and Spinal Muscular Atrophy.

For children who need physical guidance through the poses or are in a wheelchair or not ambulatory, here are some ideas to help stretch and strengthen the muscles.

If you are working with children who have spastic CP and may have certain muscles that spasm out of their control, you will want to move them slowly in and out of yoga poses. There will be times when you may not be able to move their muscles into the position you are wanting due to their muscle tone, as it can be tight.

Yoga Sequence for Children with Physical Disabilities

figure 1

- Easy Pose – deep breaths, match your breath with the child's breath to either calm them or alert them to get ready for this sequence (figure 1).
- If child is cognitively aware, practice 3 to 5 mindful breaths.
- Seated Twist Pose – this pose gently massages the abdomen. Get the child into a seated position. Sit behind him so you can help keep his hips forward and then reach his arms up high with a straight back and slowly help him twist to bring right arm behind and look over the right shoulder. Slowly return to neutral and then repeat on the other side. Hold each side for 2 to 3 breaths. You can repeat each side a few times if you like (figure 2).

figure 2

figure 3

- Butterfly Pose – help open the child's hips up into butterfly pose. If her legs do not touch the ground, hold them or place blankets or blocks under her until it's comfortable. Make sure her back is straight (figure 3).

Chapter 8: Yoga for Children Who Are Medically Fragile and/or with Physical Challenges

- Rock-n-Roll – (if you are strong enough and child is small enough) sit child in front of you and grab underneath his legs and roll him back onto you as you roll back and up. This activates the child's vestibular system. Do this 3 to 5 times (figure 4).

figure 4

- Seated Forward Bend – Sit behind the child with both legs straight out in front. Help her reach up tall and then slowly reach her arms forward towards her shins or feet. Only go as far as the child's flexibility will allow. Do not overstretch her hamstrings (figure 5).

- Head to Knee Forward Bend – Sit behind the child with both legs straight out in front. Bend the right knee in so his right foot is touching the inside of his left thigh. Help him reach up tall with a straight back and then forward fold over to his extended right leg, bending from the hips. Take the pose as far as the child's flexibility will allow. Repeat to the other side. Hold each side for 3 to 4 breaths if the child is comfortable (figure 6).

figure 5

figure 6

- Move him to his stomach (prone position).
- Cobra Pose – Help position the child's arms bent under her shoulders and then help her press up if she can, or she can stay in Sphinx Pose if that is all she can do. If the child is small enough, you can sit behind her and bring your arms underneath her shoulders and gently lift her chest and head up (figure 7).

figure 7

- Modified Bow Pose – bend the child's knees behind him, bringing his heels as close to her buttocks as you can without overstretching her quadriceps. If she can reach back and grab her feet, great, but if not, you can help her lift her head up while holding her feet (figure 8).

figure 8
(*Do not push a child too far*
into this pose)

Chapter 8: Yoga for Children Who Are Medically Fragile and/or with Physical Challenges

- Child's Pose – help move the child back so he is resting on his heels with his big toes touching. You can gently open his knees apart and either reach his arms above his head or bring them down to his sides. This should be a relaxing pose. Use this any time the child seems to be stressed or overwhelmed during yoga (figure 9).

figure 9

- Downward Dog – some children are able to maintain this pose with some help. If the child can support her weight on her arms, wrists and shoulders, you can try this with her. Do not injure yourself or the child while trying any of the poses if they are too difficult or if you have to hold too much of the child's weight (figure 10).

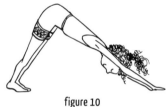

figure 10

- Roll them to their back (supine).
- Bridge Pose – bend the child's knees so his feet are flat on the floor. Gently bring your hands under his hips and help him lift his buttocks off of the floor. If his feet slip, use your leg to hold them in place. Only raise the child's bottom up as far as the child's body will allow (figure 11).

figure 11

- Happy Baby Pose (figure 12).

figure 12

- Knee to Chest Pose – this really helps children who may not move as much on their own or who face digestion issues and constipation. Remember to stretch the child's right knee first, keeping his left leg straight and then bending in his left leg with his right leg straight (figure 13).

figure 13

- Reclined Spinal Twist – make sure the child does not have any spine issues before doing this pose. Gently bend her knees into her chest and lower the knees slowly to the left side while cueing her to look to her right. Then switch sides. You can bend the child's knees at a 45-degree angle verses a 90-degree angle for a less intense stretch (figure 14).

figure 14

- Sleeping Pose – perform this pose for deep relaxation if the child will tolerate it. You can support his back by putting a bolster or blanket under his knees. You can also bend his knees up and, if needed, place a thin pillow or blanket under his head (figure 15).

figure 15

Children with Down Syndrome and Other Low Tone Challenges

Easy Pose

Down syndrome is a genetic disorder of the 21st chromosome. It also presents with a wide range of abilities in children. Most children with Down syndrome have lower muscle tone, have delayed motor skills, are of smaller stature and can have mild to significant delayed cognitive skills. They also sometimes have heart conditions. Again, yoga can be greatly beneficial to a child with Down syndrome, like any motor coordination challenge, because it helps strengthen and tone muscles and can improve overall health.

Yoga Sequence for Children with Low Tone

Make sure you are watching children who have low tone participate in yoga poses, because they can hyper-extend their muscles and joints, and it may not seem painful to them, but is not good for them. Make sure you are teaching them or helping guide them through appropriate postural positions.

1. Easy Pose (figure 1)

figure 1

2. Table Top Pose
3. Cat/Cow Pose (figure 2)

figure 2

4. Child's Pose (figure 3)

figure 3

5. Downward Dog (figure 4)

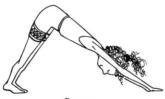

figure 4

6. Cobra Pose (figure 5)

figure 5

7. Downward Dog (figure 6)

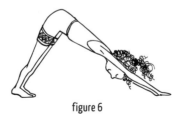

figure 6

8. Lion Pose (figure 7)

figure 7

9. Mountain Pose (figure 8)

figure 8

10. Crescent Moon Pose (figure 9)

figure 9

11. Warrior 2 Pose (figure 10)

figure 10

12. Triangle Pose (figure 11)

figure 11

13. Repeat Poses 2 to 12.
14. Easy Pose (figure 12)

figure 12

15. Rock-n-Roll (figure 13)

figure 13

16. Bridge Pose (figure 14)

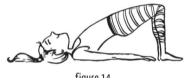

figure 14

17. Happy Baby (figure 15)

figure 15

18. Fish Pose (figure 16)

figure 16

(Make sure the child's neck is not overextended, and if they have low neck tone, only do this pose if you can help support them)

19. Sleeping Pose for Deep Relaxation (figure 17)

figure 17

Medically Fragile

Children deemed as medically fragile can indicate several different challenges and variations. Some children I work with who are determined to be medically fragile have G-tubes, a tracheostomy, seizure disorders, rare genetic syndromes, heart and kidney concerns, significant cognitive delays, and more. When you are a parent of a child who is considered medically fragile or if you are a therapist working with a child, you must make sure his doctor has cleared him to take part in yoga poses and stretches. There may be limitations to what you can and cannot do. Please make sure you are comfortable helping a child with such challenges to move safely through various yoga poses, and if you know she is unable to do a pose or will be uncomfortable doing it, skip it and choose a pose you know will benefit her and her specific needs.

Medically fragile or those with asthma—choose good poses to open the lungs and helps children who may only tolerate a few poses with slow movement.

- Cat/Cow Pose
- Butterfly Pose
- Straddle Pose

- Cobra Pose or Sphinx Pose
- Bridge Pose
- Knee to Chest Pose
- Reclined Spinal Twist
- Fish Pose
- Sleeping Pose

Yoga Sequence to Help with Digestion

Many children with autism, sensory challenges and physical disabilities have gastrointestinal issues. Some children are unable to digest certain foods, have gas pains, have trouble eating, are fed through a G-tube, etc. These poses can help a child with digestive issues, and you can help guide her through the sequence if she cannot do the poses herself. I will give additional tips regarding these poses for children with physical disabilities whom you may need to move physically through the poses. If they can imitate you and do it themselves, that's great. If they need prompting, then help them gently and safely move though the poses. If a child is non-verbal or has limited verbal skills, watch his facial expressions at all times to make sure he is comfortable.

- Child's Pose – help the child move gently into this pose and place a hand on her lower back, gently massaging their lower back (figure 1).

figure 1

Chapter 8: Yoga for Children Who Are Medically Fragile and/or with Physical Challenges

- Cat/Cow – helps contract and stretch the abdominal muscles. If the child can hold himself in Table Top Pose, you can then gently cue him to lower his stomach and hips and look up for Cow Pose and then arch his back and bring his stomach and hips up and to look down at their belly button. If possible, go through 5 rounds of breaths. If the child's arms begin to fatigue, then give him a break and come back to this pose (figure 2).

figure 2

- Downward Dog – helps relax the digestive tract (don't hold this pose too long if you or your child experiences reflux, heartburn or headache). If the child can physically hold her weight on her arms and shoulders, you can lift her hips so that her feet are pressing into the floor; this gives her a slight inversion posture. Be cautious if the child has seizures (figure 3).

figure 3

- Child's Pose (figure 4).

figure 4

- Bow Pose – Start with the child lying on his stomach. Help the child by gently bending his knees in towards his buttocks and, if possible, have him grab his feet. If he cannot lift his head off of the ground, that is okay. Be cautious if the child has a G-tube or Tracheostomy that you are not pressing on these areas while he is lying on his stomach. Hold this pose for 3 to 4 breaths (figure 5).

figure 5

- Seated Twist Pose – this pose gently massages the abdomen. Get the child into a seated position. Sit behind her so you can help keep her hips forward and then reach her arms up high with a straight back and slowly help her twist to bring the right arm behind and look over her right shoulder. Slowly return to neutral and then repeat on the other side. Hold each side for 2 to 3 breaths. You can repeat each side a few times if you like (figure 6).

figure 6

Chapter 8: Yoga for Children Who Are Medically Fragile and/or with Physical Challenges

- Head to Knee Forward Bend – Sit behind the child with both legs straight out in front. Bend the right knee in so his right foot is touching the inside of his left thigh. Help him reach up tall with a straight back and then fold forward to his extended right leg, bending from the hips. Take the pose just as far as his flexibility will allow. Repeat to the other side. Hold each side for 3 to 4 breaths if the child is comfortable (figure 7).

figure 7

- Reclined Spinal Twist Pose – Have the child lie on her back and bring both knees into her chest. Help her lower both legs over to the right side while guiding her head and left arm to the left so she gets a gentle twist. Bring her back to a neutral position, and then slowly lower her legs over to the left and gently bring her head and right arm to the right side. Do not do this if the child has back pain or scoliosis or if she is in pain during this pose. You can place a blanket under her head to make it more comfortable, and if her knees do not touch the floor, you can hold them or place a blanket underneath the knees. Hold each side for 5 breaths (figure 8).

figure 8

- Knee to Chest Pose, first Right leg (ascending colon), left leg (descending colon). You can sit in front of the child's feet while they are lying down in supine. Straighten their legs and make sure their back is aligned with their hips and shoulders. Take their right knee and bend it in while helping hold the left leg straight. Massage that right knee a little as it is bent in towards the chest and then slightly rotate out towards the armpit. Release the leg slowly and repeat on the left side. You can do this a few times on each leg to help relieve gas pain and constipation (figure 9).

figure 9

- Legs up the Wall Pose – have the child lie comfortably on his back with his bottom almost touching the wall and his legs extended up the wall. This should be relaxing, so give him a blanket under his head if needed. He can stay in this position for several minutes if he enjoys it (figure 10).

figure 10

Chapter 8: Yoga for Children Who Are Medically Fragile and/or with Physical Challenges

- Reclined Butterfly Pose – Have the child sit in butterfly pose first. Stretch her bent knees slightly to lower her legs towards the floor, but do not force them. Then slowly help her lie back in supine position, place a blanket under her head or a bolster behind her back if needed. If her bent knees do not touch the floor, place blocks or blankets under her knees or bring her feet away from the body slightly to open her legs and make the position more comfortable. She can remain in this position for a few minutes or even for deep relaxation if they like. You may also choose to move them into Sleeping Pose for deep relaxation (figure 11).

figure 11

Interview with Emily Kalmbach

Emily is currently the Adapted Physical Education teacher for all of Manhattan Beach Unified School District (MBUSD) in Manhattan Beach, Calif. She studied Kinesiology at the University of Michigan and double majored in Sports Management and Physical Education with a minor in Health. Upon graduating from U-M, she attended Cal State Long Beach for her Adapted PE credential. Emily was deeply inspired by the late Mary Norman, an APE teacher with whom she worked closely during her credential program at CSULB. She was a motivational teacher with high expectations of students, who also wanted them to be independent individuals. Prior to teaching APE for MBUSD, Emily taught general PE in the Arcadia and La Canada school districts. Emily lives in California and can be contacted at emilykalmbach@gmail.com for further questions or thoughts.

What types of children do you work with? Ages? Disabilities? What can be challenging or fun about your work with these children?

I work with children with mild/moderate to severe cognitive and physical disabilities, ranging in age from 3-22 years. Predominantly, my caseload consists of individuals with autism and Down syndrome. It is challenging to determine a child's limit in what they are capable of doing on any given day. Most of the time a child can do so much more than what the parent, teacher, aides, or even the individual thinks he/she can perform. When a child has been working on a certain skill such as shooting a basketball or jumping a rope, it is very rewarding to see the excitement on the child's face when he/she successfully completes a challenging task.

How do you use yoga techniques or therapeutic movement in your program at schools?

I use basic yoga postures with my preschool and elementary students as a way to help them stretch and strengthen and as a way to refocus them during transitions between activities. My preschool students really enjoy the different standing postures (i.e. mountain, modified eagle, and tree poses) and basic inversions (i.e. standing forward bend and downward dog).

Chapter 8: Yoga for Children Who Are Medically Fragile and/or with Physical Challenges

How do you think yoga can be used effectively in schools?

In my school district, yoga is an elective class at the high school level for the general student body. In the mild/moderate and moderate/severe special day classes the classroom teachers use yoga videos as an active break for students. Although practicing yoga via videos is a fantastic start, this population of students could really benefit from live, hands-on instruction to truly gain the physical benefits of yoga. Being able to manipulate the students' posture into correct alignment will greatly improve a child's strength, flexibility and self-confidence.

CHAPTER 9:

YOGA FOR CHILDREN WITH DEVELOPMENTAL DELAYS

Seated Forward Bend

ow do I know if my child has developmental delays?

Developmental Delay (DD) is a term used to describe a child who is behind in one or more areas of development, such as gross or fine motor skills, language skills and/or cognitive skills. When children are young, they may show a global developmental delay because they are not yet meeting their developmental milestones on time and need therapy to help progress on those milestones.

In schools, this terminology is used to describe a child who qualifies for an Individualized Education Plan IEP) based on his or her delays regarding academic skills, motor skills and language skills. Each state has different qualifications on the qualifications a child must meet for an IEP in the school to receive support in their classroom. Many children receive a label of DD when they are young, but with OT, PT and/or Speech Therapy, they may "catch up" to their same-age peers and no longer need services. Other children end up getting a more accurate diagnosis as they get older, like Learning Disabilities (LD), ADD, ASD, SPD, Cognitive Impairment, or other diagnoses that may have affected their motor development. Currently, children cannot qualify for an IEP with a Sensory Processing Disorder diagnosis. They must be eligible for school-based services under whatever state and district guidelines there are for that specific area, and they all differ slightly.

If you have a child with DD and they are also affected cognitively, make sure you are catering their teaching to their developmental level, not their chronological age. That means that, if a child is 6 years old but is showing the skills of a 3 year old, you should adjust your approach with them to what you expect out of a 3 year old. They may not sit and participate for as long as other 6 year olds would in a yoga class or sequence; they may need more visuals or explanation of poses in order to understand them. They may need more time to figure out the motor pattern if their motor skills are delayed. You do not have to expect children to perform perfectly, but adopt realistic expectations for them. We expect too little from some children, and if we do not challenge them enough, they may begin to goof off or act out. Make sure you know your child/student and can give them that just-right challenge.

Yoga Sequences for Children with DD

Any of the above-listed sequences could work for a child with developmental delays, physical motor delays or cognitive delays. For a child with physical motor delays, simplify the yoga sequence and make sure you are gently guiding children into the correct positions so they do not hurt themselves. Use your judgment based on the child's specific needs to move through the yoga poses slowly and help model for them and give them time to move through them.

For a child with a cognitive delay, simplify the yoga sequence and give them visuals to use if they are visual learners. If the child cannot tolerate more than five poses, start there and slowly teach them and then build on those poses as they continue to practice. You may need to break down even the simple poses into parts and teach them individually before they try to move into a sequence.

CHAPTER 10:

YOGA FOR PARENTS AND CAREGIVERS

Triangle Pose

Chapter 10: Yoga for Parents and Caregivers

If you are a parent or caregiver of a child with special needs, you know first-hand how stressful it can be. I do not have a child of my own with special needs, but because my younger sister has a disability, I can somewhat relate to situations that such families face. I know there can be a grieving process upon discovering that your child has been diagnosed with special needs. Sometimes a family can face multiple medical challenges, behavioral concerns, academic and social challenges and more.

As parents/caregivers, you must make sure you are taking care of yourself so that you can have the energy and compassion to take care of your child. Practicing yoga with your child is a great strategy, but you also need to have your own time and activities. Practice yoga on your own, practice mindfulness, have date night, get a massage, work out or do whatever helps you make time for yourself.

Now you may think that this task is impossible. Where are you going to find time for yourself or have a date night with your partner/spouse? I know it is hard to find a decent nanny or babysitter to watch your child, but it is especially difficult if you have a child with special needs. There are many respite programs out there that can help provide a caregiver that can support your specific child's needs, whether behavioral or medical needs, G-tube feeding, medication administration, etc. Many early intervention programs offer family support and respite care, and there are other programs that offer similar support. Some families have grandparents or other family members that could offer to help out one night a month for date night or allow you to attend a yoga class. Maybe you and your spouse or partner can take turns having a break during the week so you each can engage in a special activity for yourselves.

When thinking about mindfulness and encouraging your child or the children you work with to pay attention to their own bodies, breathing, minds, etc., we as adults, therapists and caregivers should also apply the same advice to ourselves. Just as it is important for parents and caregivers to make sure they are caring for themselves, therapists and teachers who work with students with or without special needs should make sure they are taking care of their own needs. Try taking a new perspective on life, engaging in positive thinking, practicing mindfulness and being aware of your present situation and making each day count.

As someone who has normal day-to-day stress from the home, family stress and the addition of work stress of working multiple jobs, caring for children with varying types and degrees of special needs, I need to continue to make yoga, therapeutic movement and mindfulness a part of my everyday life. I have most recently adapted a new mind-set (not that I haven't tried to do this in the past, but trying to make this more of a habit in my life) regarding being mindful, being present, positive thinking, and tending to the health of my mind, body and spirit. I can only imagine an additional stress of raising a child with special needs, and I want every parent/caregiver out there to try to make a small change in their own lives and have a positive influence on their child's life. This is your new challenge!

CHAPTER 11:

YOGA IN SCHOOLS

From top to bottom: Sphinx Pose, Yoga Group Relaxation, and Mountain Pose

Chapter 11: Yoga in Schools

Yoga in schools is definitely a growing trend across the country. Many school districts prefer that the term "yoga" be replaced with something different. You can refer to it as Therapeutic Movement, Mindfulness, etc. As we talked about earlier, yoga is not a religion, and we want to make sure parents feel comfortable with the programs we offer in the classroom. You can still use the same techniques we have talked about in this book and the English terminology for poses and postures with your students in a school setting. If you are a teacher, therapist or aide in the classroom and you are trained and knowledgeable about yoga and body mechanics, you can use these techniques. As we disclaimed before, make sure you know each child well, make sure you have parent permission, and make sure you are comfortable helping guide a child through their "therapeutic postures." As an occupational therapist who works in a school district, I see children individually or in a small group setting as part of their Individualized Education Plan (IEP). If they have a goal regarding sensory regulation, attention, fine motor, handwriting, core strength, etc., I can build these therapeutic sequences into my OT time for them, which then helps them meet their IEP goals.

Many teachers in classrooms are using movement breaks or "brain breaks" in their classroom to get their children up and moving. They are also using breathing techniques to help calm the students down before testing after a busy day or whenever they see the students need a break. We know that movement improves our learning, but we also need to know how to use movement appropriately and safely for all children in the classroom. Some types of movements will rev their engines up, and some will calm them down. Some activities, for example, will calm Johnny but rev up Sarah. Be flexible and observe your students in the classroom to determine what is best for them during that movement in time; many times this involves trial and error.

I know that teachers will say, "I do not have time to pack in one extra thing into my already busy day," but if you look at the research, practicing some movement, brain break or mindfulness activity will improve the students' focus, attention and work production. One study reports that mindful awareness practice improved executive functioning in elementary school-aged children (Flook, L. 2010). I know it can overwhelm a teacher or staff member to think about adding one more thing to their already busy day, but these things can take just a few short minutes in your day and can really change the culture and attitude of the children in the classroom.

Therapeutic Activities You Can Do from Your Desk

There are plenty of things that children can do individually or as a group even from their desk. Once we teach children about the various breathing techniques and how to be "mindful" they can be easily cued on strategies and eventually will utilize them on their own. A child can easily practice any of the calming breathing techniques sitting in their chair without bringing too much attention to themselves. He or she can also participate in activities that help with waking his/her brain up but keeping him/her focused, like the following:

- Doing chair push-ups
- Squeezing hands together
- Leaning forward and resting chin in your hand

- Marching the feet quietly
- Stretching arms up overhead
- Tying stretchy band around the bottom of his/her chair for the feet to push on to get movement/input
- Sitting on a wiggle cushion if it helps keep him/her focused
- Chewing gum if he/she can do so safely and responsibly
- Drinking from a water bottle (sports water top or CamelBak is good)

Then if a group can take part in some movement, breathing exercises you can have them participate in any of the mindfulness activities, any of the above listed chair activities, or get them up and doing therapeutic movement or the yoga sequences.

Make sure kids have enough room to move and stretch, and make sure they are being safe and that you are not giving them anything too challenging to do. A more active movement break might look like this:

- 10 jumping jacks
- Touching finger to nose with eyes closed
- Balancing on one foot (Tree Pose)
- Hopping on one foot for 5 hops, then repeating on the other foot
- Cross crawls (taking the right elbow and bending the left knee up to touch it and then bringing the left elbow to the right knee)
- Push 5s with a partner (find a friend put your hands up in a high-10 position and pressing evenly against each other to give heavy work feedback to the body
- 10 wall push-ups
- Side step, tap foot, side step, tap foot
- Grapevine

- Turning 3 times to the right, turn 3 times to the left
- Slowing down and reach overhead, leaning forward and touch toes
- Taking 3 slow deep breaths and sitting back in chair

Giving your students movement breaks, sensory breaks or brain breaks (whatever you want to call them) will keep their brains active, keep them from falling asleep and shutting down, or giving fidgety kids the opportunity to move and get that needed input in a structured way. All of these ideas will help improve attention and focus, and though it takes 3-5 minutes out of your day, the children will be more focused in the long run.

Mindful Life™ Training in Schools

Kristen Race, Ph.D., is the creator and founder of Mindful Life™. She travels all over the country, training schools, camps, businesses, parents and after-school programs about this amazing program. Mindful Life's mission is to provide as many children and adults as possible with simple solutions to our complicated lives. Her program addresses stress and how much it affects our brains. The prefrontal cortex of the brain handles problem solving, executive functioning, attention, processing of positive emotions and most classroom learning occurs. Dr. Race calls this the "smart part" of our brain. When we become stressed, the part of our brain that processes that emotion is the amygdala. This is where our fight, flight or freeze reactions come from (see Chapter 1 on SPD for more information). The amygdala controls our emotions—happy, sad, mad, silliness, fear, stress, etc. When our bodies and minds become more stressed, we trigger pathways to the amygdala part of our brain (Dr. Race calls this the "alarm" part of our brain), and this is sometimes a stronger response than that of our prefrontal cortex. For example, you may have a close encounter while driving in a car and almost getting hit, your fear and stress response goes into a heightened state, and you may not access as much of your problem solving skills and executive functioning in that moment, which causes you to react in a more emotional level. Some children may consistently be in fight, flight or freeze mode because their sensory nervous systems are overwhelmed, and instead of making a rationale decision when their teacher asks them to pull out their math homework, they may throw a temper tantrum that is not age appropriate.

Mindfulness strengthens those pathways to the prefrontal cortex so we are better armed to deal with stress, fear, anxiety and frustration. When I am teaching parents about sensory regulation and how we want our bodies to stay in our just-right zone, I use the following example: think of a time when you woke up late because your alarm didn't go off, your coffee machine was broken, your child was crying and refused to get dressed for school, you hurried to work, and when you get to the office you realized that you were supposed to present at the staff meeting and you did not have your presentation ready to go. I think in this case, your amygdala is in full hijack at this point. How in the world would you calm yourself down? How do you think our children feel when we put so much on their plate? Their stress and anxiety increase so much that they also reach this point of amygdala hijack. This is where we need to teach our children about Mindful Body, Mindful Listening, Mindful Breathing, and Mindful Eating.

Mindful Life™ Programs are rooted in the science of the brain:

- They integrate cognitive neuroscience and positive psychology in the field of mindfulness

- They show how the brain functions under different conditions (alarm brain vs. smart brain)
- They provide insight into how to maximize attention, efficiency and productivity
- They help you become healthier, happier and more resilient to the stress in your life

Dr. Race teaches how to prepare your body for mindfulness. This can include sitting cross-legged on the floor with hands on knees and a straight back with relaxed shoulders; you should be comfortable. A position in preparation for mindfulness can also be sitting in a chair with both feet flat on the floor and your hands on your knees without crossing hands or feet and your back straight but with relaxed shoulders. Mindful Listening is hearing a sound of a tone bar and listening for as long as you can with your eyes closed, or listening for the furthest sound you can hear, focusing your energy and brain on your active listening. Then she talks about Mindful Breathing, which we discussed earlier as being aware of your breath, and we have also talked about ways to challenge yourself with different breaths. Dr. Race then describes Mindful Eating as eating healthy and being aware of what you are putting into your body as something that affects our whole brain and nervous system. We know that everything is connected, so it's only natural for us to want to make sure we are providing our bodies with the best types of foods we can, including proteins, fresh fruits and vegetables and less processed foods that are easy to make out of a box.

Kristen Race, Ph.D., is a parent of two young children and an expert in child, family and school psychology. Dr. Race is the author of *Mindful*

Parenting and founder of Mindful Life™. All of her programs are rooted in the science of the brain, with influences from the fields of mindfulness and positive psychology. Mindful Life programs improve brain function and brain development in adults and children.

Dr. Race has been featured in *The New York Times*, NPR, *The Washington Post*, *Chicago Tribune*, *USA TODAY*, CNN, and *Real Simple Magazine*. She is a regular blogger for *The Huffington Post* and *Psychology Today*. She is a TEDx and keynote speaker and has trained over 10,000 leaders in her methods worldwide.

Dr. Race received her Doctorate and Master's degrees from the University of Denver and her Bachelor's degree from the University of Colorado. She resides in Steamboat Springs, Colorado, where she can be found mountain biking, hiking, playing soccer, and chasing her kids down the ski mountain!

CHAPTER 12:

PRACTICING YOGA WITH YOUR CHILD/ THERAPISTS USING YOGA AS A THERAPEUTIC TOOL

Supported Handstand

Chapter 12: Practicing Yoga with Your Child/Therapists Using Yoga as a Therapeutic Tool

For those of us out there who are already occupational, physical or motor therapists, these ideas are familiar to us. You can take the yoga sequences, the mindfulness and the movement breaks and incorporate them into your already developed practice. I am sure you already use some sensory strategies with your children, and I know you are considering implementing core strengthening and postural control with those kids who need it. You may decide that in some therapy sessions you will do a whole yoga or therapeutic movement sequence and in another session you will work on sensory integration on the swing, trampoline and therapy ball. The more I think about being mindful and using my own calming strategies for myself, the more I utilize those strategies in my therapy sessions and the better my therapeutic outcomes are.

For those of you who are yoga teachers and have a yoga background but are trying to learn more about children with special needs, hopefully this book has helped provide you some information, but mostly it will take time, experience and more knowledge to figure out what types of yoga poses, sequences, etc., will work for that specific kiddo. You may have a whole list of different idea for a child you see because you know him or her better; that's great. I encourage therapists to use their skills and seek other experts in the field to help them build on their current practice as a growing therapist.

Parents and caregivers, I hope this book has offered you some ideas on how to incorporate yoga, therapeutic movement, mindfulness and more methods into your child's daily routine. The amount of therapies some children receive can be overwhelming, and parents have a lot on their plate. I encourage you to try out these methods and see what works best for your child. If something is not right or is not working well, trial and error can be a good strategy. You can also seek a trained therapist or yoga instructor to specifically design a therapy program that fits your child's needs. If things are working and you are seeing positive changes, great! Again, do not forget that you are supposed to also be taking care of you and your needs, so you have the emotional availability and energy to care for your child. Good luck, and I wish you all the best!

Interview with Roxanne Naseem Rashedi

Roxanne has been a yoga practitioner since 2000 and an instructor since 2009. She is currently a PhD student in Education at UC Davis and is conducting research at the M.I.N.D. Institute. She holds an MA from Georgetown University and a BA from UC Berkeley. Roxanne has earned a 240-hour certification in Flow Yoga and is pursuing her 500-hour certification.

Roxanne is involved in a yoga project with at-risk pre-schoolers with ADHD. As an educator, Roxanne is interested in exploring yoga as a tool to help both atypically and typically developing children manage their emotions and focus their attention in academic and non-academic settings.

How do you see yoga benefitting children with special needs?

This is an interesting question! Depending on the child's particular needs, I think that the potential benefits of yoga can vary greatly. In a recent literature review, Schmalzl, Powers, and Blom (2015) reported that yoga may more efficiently increase interoceptive and proprioceptive awareness and general attentional skills when practicing seated meditation. I believe that yoga can create more space for a child to better relate to his/her emotions in real-time.

Can you describe what you mean by relating to emotions? Is that similar to emotion regulation?

Yes. I think emotion regulation is a broad term that gets used frequently in numerous fields. Dacher Keltner, a professor of psychology, has written on emotions and shows how each emotion has a specific purpose in a particular context (Keltner and Shiota, 2003). For example, contentment could function as a sense of feeling fulfilled. In this sense, we could refer to the process of relating to emotion because it creates space for a child to recognize, sit with and understand their emotions instead of trying to quickly suppress and/or control them. This may get tricky, especially when the child experiences negative emotions while practicing yoga. Educators and parents may be concerned that a negative emotion could escalate into a meltdown. However, yoga practices may show a child that negative emotions are part of the experience both on and off the mat. And on the mat, the child can fully and safely experience these negative emotions with each calming, deliberate breath.

So would you say that one benefit of yoga for children with special needs is being more sensitive to emotions?

Definitely. Rather than suppressing emotions and/or reacting to them immediately, yoga can help children with special needs breathe and move through their emotions. This sensitivity could be broken down into parts, focused attention (FA) and open monitoring (OM), the former being more for novice practitioners, while the latter is associated with more experienced practitioners (Schmalzl et al., 2015). In FA, a child would be asked to direct and sustain their attention on a single object (e.g., the length of their breath), whereas in OM, a child would monitor his or her thoughts in a yoga flow, without becoming attached to any thought or sensation (Schmalzl et al., 2015).

I like to think of the yoga shapes (i.e., asanas) as vehicles through which a child will develop awareness of what sensations surface. A child can use the breath and learn how to pay attention to his or her own body. The child learns strategies that best navigate his or her way through the experience. Thus, the yoga practice is not something that a child "does" or something checked off a to-do list. "The yoga practice is a practice for a life, a tool that the child can turn to on the playground, in the classroom, or in any stressful situation. In this sense, practicing on the yoga mat becomes a symbolic space for a child to explore, challenge, and better gain learning strategies not only for the yoga shapes, but also for all the kinds of shapes and situations that the child will encounter off the mat and in life."

Is there research that examines the relationship between yoga, emotions, and children with special needs?

Yes, there is a growing body of literature examining contemplative practices (e.g., yoga, mindful eating, mindful breathing) as tools to teach children with and without special needs about social emotional learning (Shapiro, Lyons, Miller, Butler, Vieten, and Zelazo, 2014). However, much of the literature to date is exploratory in nature, with small sample sizes and non-randomized designs (Shapiro et al., 2014). Consequently, the findings do not generalize to the population in which the researchers aim to learn more about.

However, studies have reported that children with special needs experienced more challenges in peer relationships and social adjustment (Kavale and Mostert, 2004). Mindfulness practices like yoga have been shown to enhance peer relationships and reduce anxiety levels for these special populations (Harrison, Manocha, & Rubia, 2004). Overall, yoga has served as a complementary treatment for children with special needs and has helped improve their ability to relate to their emotions in a focused, caring manner (Shapiro et al., 2014).

What have some of these studies reported?

One study that comes to mind (Harrison et al., 2004) was a joint child and parent intervention. The researchers used the Sahaja Yoga Meditation (SYM) program as a supplementary treatment for children with ADHD. The study lasted six weeks and consisted of 90-minute sessions that took place twice a week at a hospital. Participants also engaged in regular meditation practices at home. The meditation practice asked both parents and children to enter a state of non-judgmental awareness. Interventionists helped participants become aware of this state by modeling silence and directing their attention inward. Starting in Week 4, one of the weekly meditation sessions involved both the parent and child. The intention was for the interventionist to help train parents to facilitate their child's meditation at home. Results showed significant improvements in the children's ADHD behavior and increased self-esteem and peer relations. Children reported benefits in their sleeping patterns and feeling less anxious at school. Improved academic concentration was reported, and parents reported feeling better able to manage their child's behavior.

This sounds promising. Could there be any drawbacks?

It sounds promising, but like other studies in this field, the authors had a small sample size. In fact, a Cochrane review (2010) of four studies evaluated meditation interventions for children with ADHD and was unsuccessful in their attempts to draw conclusions; this was mainly due to the small sample sizes of these studies. Additionally, the SYM study did not include a control group, and their findings may be biased since there was a high dropout rate. Many of the significant results were based on parent-rated questionnaires; consequently, parents may have wished to present their caretaking abilities and children in a solely positive light. Children also self-reported their self-esteem scores and reported high scores at both time-points, and we have to consider that it may be difficult to interpret these self-reports reliably.

Another drawback I noticed in this growing body of research and in the SYM program was that the program itself was not described in detail. For instance, how did the interventionist model open awareness? In what ways did the interventionist help train parents to guide their child through meditation practices? We don't have the answers to these questions. I would also add that the SYM program appeared to include a strictly meditative component, and not an asana (yogic) aspect. Future research may incorporate mindful movement (asana) and breathing techniques to see if children benefit more in one kind of treatment group.

Chapter 12: Practicing Yoga with Your Child/Therapists Using Yoga as a Therapeutic Tool

Can you describe an example of what this incorporation of breath and asana might look like on the mat for a child with special needs?

Sure. So, let's say we are working with a child who lives by repetitive, rigid routines. Consequently, the yoga practice could be become a crutch, especially if a child moves through the same set of asanas with relative ease. This is why the teacher/therapist needs to implement the intervention/practice in a deliberate, personalized way. The child who thrives on routine may benefit greatly from practicing just one or two new asanas or even a different transition into an asana. These subtle changes can help build new networks and patterns of behavior. Even though the child may show resistance upon starting the practice in child's pose instead of mountain pose, for example, the teacher/therapist can show the child how to use deep breaths to face this resistance head on. With each breath, the child learns how to strengthen his or her own vagal tone and can explore these minor changes with great curiosity rather than approaching novelty with resistance and aggression, for instance.

Can you describe vagal tone as it applies to teaching yoga to children with special needs?

I like to think of the vagus nerve as the body's engine of resilience and affiliation. The tenth cranial nerve, the vagus nerve, is an essential part of parasympathetic nervous system (PNS) and mediates changes in heart rate (Porges, Doussard-Roosevelt, & Mait, 1994). Vagal tone refers to the activity of this nerve and regulates the rest and digest state of much of the body's internal organ systems, including the lungs and heart (Porges et al., 1994). Since yoga postures emphasize strengthening the core muscles as well

---

as activating interior muscles, peripheral vagal stimulation is enhanced (Schmalzl et al., 2015).

Moreover, the yoga practice exposes a child to physically challenging postures, and these postures sometimes evoke a variety of sensations and emotions. However, the child has an opportunity to continually embody these postures with a calm, rhythmic breath; over time, a child can gain the ability to remain calm during a possible stressful experience (Schmalzl et al., 2015). Thus, it has been speculated that yoga practices can help create an internal sense of calmness for the child and increase parasympathetic activation and self-regulatory behaviors (Schmalzl et al., 2015). Ideally, I would imagine that one intention of the yoga practice would be for the child to transfer the strategies from the yoga mat off the mat and into the playground, at school, and so forth. Children and adults alike can strengthen their vagal tone by taking slow, diaphragmatic breaths – usually 5 to 6 breaths per minute. In the scenario described above, a child can learn how to calmly practice new asanas or transitions by learning how to take slow, diaphragmatic breaths. In effect, the child strengthens his/her vagal tone.

So for children who are over-responsive or in a flight or fight sensory pattern, what asanas or breathing techniques are best to help calm them down?

It depends on the child, and each case could be different. I would advise the use of asanas that balance the sympathetic nervous system (SNS) by accessing its counterpart, the parasympathetic nervous system (PNS). You would want to design a sequence that integrates both ease and steadiness. In other words, you should consider including asanas that are characterized as hypertonic (e.g., chair pose, or poses that require a high level of muscular tension) and hypotonic (e.g., reclining butterfly pose or other poses that require less muscular tension); by doing so, you help create a practice that cultivates well-balanced tension (Alexander, 1985). Creating a flow that incorporates both stability and strength is essential, but it is important to encourage the child to take deep inhales and exhales; this helps activate the PNS and support deeper respiration. To name a few, forward fold poses such as standing forward fold, child's pose, and seated forward bend aid in calming a child's over-responsive sensory pattern.

Interview with Molly Grove

Molly Grove is a yoga therapist who specializes in working with children and adults with special needs. She studied yoga at the Sivananda Yoga Ashram in India, trained under Sonia Sumar, and is a Yoga Alliance certified yoga teacher. She received her Masters of Arts in Journalism and Mass Communications at Marshall University where she was a Division 1 track and field athlete. She has taught yoga to children and adults with special needs in India, Thailand, and the United States. Molly's yoga therapy practice is currently based in Denver, CO and her website is www. grovetreeyoga.com.

What is it like studying yoga in India, where most of this practice started?

Studying yoga in India was eye opening. In the western world, yoga is typically viewed as physical exercise. However, during my study in India, I realized that yoga not only encompasses the physical side of a person but can also access their mental and emotionally side. Studying there helped me better understand how yoga can be developed and integrated daily to help improve a person's quality of life.

In what other countries have you studied yoga?

I studied Hatha yoga extensively at the Sivananda Yoga Ashram in India, and since training there, I have practiced and taught yoga in India, Thailand, Spain and the United States.

What was your experience like working with children in the orphanages?

In India I worked at five different Catholic orphanages; three of them were homes/boarding houses for children ages 3 to 18, and the other two were orphanages/homes/schools for individuals with special needs or disabilities from age 3 to 67. Each location differed vastly from the other, and the way the children were treated at certain locations was devastating. As in most third-world countries, the resources available to the children were minimal, if present at all. Most of the locations had four to eight nuns/brothers and anywhere from 50 to 100 children.

Yoga therapy is very accessible to bring into these locations because there is no overhead or continual cost, and that was a huge factor towards the nuns' acceptance of the implementation. There are many ways to integrate yoga into the lives of individuals with special needs, and each has their own benefit. When working at one of the homes/schools, I taught an inclusive group class to over 60 individuals, all with varying needs. In that setting, I offered modifications and encouraged breath work and effort. In a class that large, I had to ensure that I met the students where they were and acknowledged their presence and their effort in class. Due to the size of the class, yoga provided a sense of safety and inclusion among the students. For example, many of the students who were non-verbal and typically could not maintain a singular focus found themselves participating because they observed the movement of their peers, which made them included and worthy.

At the second location, I was able to work one on one with children, and this produced amazing results. Yoga is not only a physical practice but also a very mental and emotional one. For children who have never felt love or hope, the physical contact and connection that is provided during one-on-one therapy is transformative. Upon combining it with other forms of sensory therapy, such as sound and light therapy, the children can blossom. I worked at those two locations for six months, and when I went back a year later, the students still remembered what I had taught, and they shared it and taught it back to me.

What type of results have you seen in your time practicing yoga therapy?

Over the past three years, I have worked with children and adults of all ages and abilities, and in as little as six months, major changes can occur. When working in the orphanages for individuals with special needs, I saw children crawl who had never been able to support themselves, I observed children with autism become more internally aware of themselves and their emotions and become externally more comfortable in group settings. I witnessed children who were deemed unresponsive and who had no hope learn to recognize my voice, clap along to songs, and lengthen and relax muscles with hypertonia. I believe that one-on-one yoga therapy combined with social integration of group classes increases the quality of life for children with special needs.

What types of disabilities did you see while you were there, and how do you think yoga can help those children?

While working in orphanages, I rarely knew how or when a child was diagnosed. Because I did not have access to their medical records, which could have provided me more information, I had the benefit of working with them without any preconceived notions of their ability or potential. I worked with them where they were and respected their boundaries, but I also didn't put a limit on what they could accomplish or how they could develop and grow. Having previous knowledge and experience with individuals with special needs, I observed that some of the children I worked with showed signs similar to those children with Cerebral Palsy, Auditory Processing Disorder, Autism Spectrum Disorder, Down syndrome, visual impairment, epilepsy, muscular dystrophy, spina bifida, and global developmental delays. Yoga therapy improved the quality of life in each of the children with whom I worked.

Interview with Heather Foerster-Bach, MOT, OTR/L, RYT

Heather found yoga in 1994 when she first stepped onto a mat for a college elective. Her experience was powerful and she has continued on the yoga path ever since. Heather has had an opportunity to practice and learn from an amazing group of teachers. In 2005, she completed a 200-hour level certification.

As a Pediatric Occupational Therapist, Heather has focused on bringing yoga to children both through her work and within the community. She believes in empowering children to find that place of calm and playfulness, and then generalize that power into their everyday life.

Chapter 12: Practicing Yoga with Your Child/Therapists Using Yoga as a Therapeutic Tool

As an OT and a Yoga Instructor, how do you incorporate yoga into your therapy practice?

Most often I can use yoga techniques in the beginning of my session because it's grounding and helps the children focus. I choose poses that will tie into what I am working on in the session. This really helps the kids with self-regulation. School demands have changed so drastically, so many kids are overwhelmed, stressed anxious, and I believe yoga is the answer to many of their issues. Yoga teaches them strategies they can do on their own, even while in class.

I start with various yoga poses like arm balances, poses that require weight bearing though arms and legs, then balance poses and then transition to handwriting or feeding therapy, if I am at the hospital. I find these kids can then sit and focus on the difficult task that I am trying to teach them.

Do you work one-on-one with students or in a group setting? When teaching yoga to children with special needs, is it difficult to teach in a large group?

It depends on the child. I like to do yoga in a group because it builds a rapport with everyone and they can learn from each other. We are playful in how we do the group. I will have from 6 to 7 kids and their abilities may range from SPD, ASD, ADHD, Bipolar disorder, etc. It is a vast group but I tell them, you never have to do anything you don't want to, you just have to try and watch your friends. I offer one pose or three poses a day, and then build on that as they become more interested in the group activity. I will put out a visual cue for them to try three different poses one day if they are having a hard time. Sometimes we will do animal walks around the room and pretend we are in the jungle. These pictures can be on cards to help them visually. I never want them to feel like I am forcing them, that defeats the purpose of yoga. Many of my kids will participate in the relaxation at the end of the group and this is still a great benefit for them.

It is a great idea to give them a mat to define their space and even if they watch and observe the other children, that is enough. I also use partner yoga poses with straps and fun props. The kids really like this because they can do the poses together.

It can be difficult and stressful to work with and/or parent a child with special needs. How has yoga personally helped you grow as a professional in this field?

It is so important! I don't think I could do what I do for a living without my yoga practice. I can tell when I am not practicing enough; I get more irritable, less patient. Working with children with special needs (and parenting a child with special needs) can be so intense and what these kids go through, it's a lot and you take on a lot when working with this population. When you are working with a child that is very dysregulated, it makes it harder if you are not regulated yourself. The minute I do downward dog or any heavy work type of pose, I can just breathe and let it out. Then I feel that I can be there for others and for my own family. I also feel I can then be more receptive to the parents to help support them with what they are going through.

Chapter 12: Practicing Yoga with Your Child/Therapists Using Yoga as a Therapeutic Tool

What other advice do you have for therapists and/or parents?

I focus on children with Autism Spectrum Disorder and psychiatric issues in a lot of my work. I focus on breathing and being in control of our own bodies. I teach the kids that we can do this in the grocery store line, or take a break to the bathroom and do a yoga pose. They also can do a balancing pose in line while waiting. I use the breathing ball a lot with a child that has Autism Spectrum Disorder. When you show them this ball, they have such a good visual of this that once they learn it, they can use this strategy even with they don't have it in front of them because usually they are great visual learners.

I have taught yoga in each of my child's classrooms and it was well received. I explain to the kids how yoga helps and how we need to calm and focus our bodies. I show them some ideas for chair yoga—stretches overhead, bending to one side, then the opposite side. I show them warrior arms out front, one leg over the chair, and stretch the back leg out. They can also place their heads on their desk and close their eyes and listen to their breathing or place their hands on their belly and take deep breaths.

ENDNOTES

1. Collins, B. & Olson, J.L. (2012) *Sensory Parenting: The Elementary Years.* Arlington, TX: Future Horizons.

2. Retrieved January 15, 2015 from http://en.wikipedia.org/wiki/Yoga

3. Retrieved January 15, 2015 from www.americanyogaassociation.org

4. Retrieved February 6, 2015 from www.americanyogaassociation.org

5. Retrieved February 6, 2015 from http://www.yogajournal.com/category/poses/types/pranayama

6. Retrieved August 1, 2015 from http://greatergood.berkeley.edu/topic/mindfulness/definition
Davidson, R.J., Kabat-Zinn, J., Schumacher, J., Rosenkranz, M., Muller, D., Santorelli, S.F., Urbanowski, F., Harrington, A., Bonus, K., & Sheridan, J. F. (2003) Alterations in Brain and Immune Function Produced by Mindfulness Meditation. *Psychosomatic Medicine, 65,* 564–570. doi:10.1097/01.PSY.0000077505.67574.E3

7. Retrieved August 5, 2015 from http://www.livingwell.org.au/mindfulness-exercises-3/5-breathing-mindfulness

8. Retrieved August 5, 2015 from http://www.mayoclinic.org/diseases-conditions/adhd/basics/definition/con-20023647

REFERENCES

http://www.ninds.nih.gov/disorders/cerebral_palsy/cerebral_palsy.htm
National Institute of Neurological Disorders and Stroke

Barnes, P. M., Bloom, B., & Nahin, R. (2008). Complementary and alternative medicine use among adults and children: United States 2007. *CDC National Health Statistics Report*, 12, 1-4.

Goldberg, L. (2004). Creative relaxation: A yoga-based program for regular and exceptional student education. *International Journal of Yoga Therapy*, 14, 68–78. Retrieved from www.relaxationnow.net/articles/exceptionaled.html

Flook, L. (2010) Effects of Mindful Awareness Practices on Executive Functions in Elementary School Children. *Journal of Applied School Psychology*, 23: 1, 70-95.

Lane, S.J., Reynolds, S., & Dumenci, L. (2012). Sensory over-responsivity and anxiety in typical children and children with Autism and Attention Deficit Hyperactivity Disorder: Cause or co-existence? *American Journal of Occupational Therapy*, 66 (5), 595-603.

https://www.academia.edu/3145421/The_Acute_Effects_of_Yoga_on_Executive_Function (Referenced June 30, 2015)

Interview with Amber Waheed, PhD

References:

Lazar, S., Singleton, O., Holzel, B., Vangel, M., Brach, N. & Carmody, J. (2014). Change in Brainstem Gray Matter Concentration Following a

Mindfulness-Based Intervention is Correlated with Improvement in Psychological Well-Being. *Frontiers in Human Neuroscience*, 8, 33.

Peck, H., Kehle, T., Bray, M. & Theodore, L. (2005). Yoga as Intervention for Children with Attention Problems. *School Psychology Review*, 34(3), 415-424.

Steeter, C., Whitfield, T., Own, L., Rein, T., Karri, S., Yakhind, A., Perlmutter, R., Prescott, A., Renshaw, C., & Jensen, E. (2010). Effects of Yoga Versus Walking on Mood, Anxiety & Brain GABA Levels: A Randomized Controlled MRS Study. *Journal of Alternative and Complementary Medicine*, 16(11), 1145-1152.

Telles, S., Gaur, V., Balkrishna, A. (2009). Effect of a Yoga session and a yoga theory session on state anxiety. *Perceptual and Motor Skills*, 109. 924-930.

Interview with Roxanne Naseem Rashedi

References:

Alexander, G. (1985). *Eutony: The Holistic Discovery of the Total Person.* Great Neck, NY: Felix Morrow.

Harrison, L., Manocha, R., Rubia, K. (2004). Sahaja yoga meditation as a family treatment programme for children with attention deficit-hyperactivity disorder. *Clinical Child Psychology and Psychiatry*, 9(4), 479-97.

Kavale, K., & Mostert, M. (2004). Social skills interventions for individuals with learning disabilities. *Learning Disability Quarterly*, 27, 31-42.

References

Keltner, D., & Shiota, M. N. (2003). New displays and new emotions: A commentary on Rozin and Cohen. *Emotion, 3,* 86-91.

Krisanaprakornkit, T., Ngamjarus, C., Witoonchart, C., et al. (2010). Meditation therapies for attention- deficit/hyperactivity disorder (ADHD). *Cochrane Database of Systematic Reviews, 6.* DOI: 10.1002/14651858.CD006507.pub2.

Porges, S., Doussard-Roosevelt, J., & Mait, A. (1994). Vagal tone and the physiological regulation of emotion. *Monographs of the Society for Research in Child Development, 59*(3), 167-186.

Schamlzl, L., Powers, C., & Henje Blom, E. (2015). Neurophysiological and neurocognitive mechanisms underlying the effects of yoga-based practices: toward a comprehensive theoretical framework. *Frontiers in Neuroscience, 9,* 1-19.

Shapiro, S., Lyons, K., Miller, R., Butler, B., Vieten, C., & Zelazo, P. (2014). Contemplation in the Classroom: a New Direction for Improving Childhood Education. *Edu Psychol Rev, 27,* 1-30.

RESOURCES

1. www.yogajournal.com

2. www.sensoryparenting.com

3. *Get Ready to Learn School Program*, by Anne Buckley-Reen OTR/L RYT — http://home.getreadytolearn.net/

4. *Yoga for the Special Child*, by Sonia Sumar

5. *Yoga Therapy for Children with Autism and Special Needs*, by Louise Goldberg

6. Yoga Alliance — https://www.yogaalliance.org/

7. Children's Yoga Teacher Training Collaborative — http://childrensyogattc.com/

8. Every Kids Yoga — www.everykidsyoga.com (Craig Hanauer RYT Training Programs for Children with Special Needs)

9. Mindful Life™ — www.mindfullifetoday.com, Kristen Race, PhD

10. Zones of Regulation — www.zonesofregulation.com

ABOUT THE AUTHOR

Pediatric Occupational Therapist Britt Collins graduated from Colorado State University over 10 years ago and since then has worked tirelessly in OT and Sensory Integration awareness, research, and application. Britt has worked in a variety of settings, including pediatric hospital inpatient units, ICU, rehabilitation, outpatient clinics, homes, schools, and skilled nursing facilities. Her award-winning OT DVD series and two books—*Sensory Parenting: Newborns to Toddlers* and *Sensory Parenting: The Elementary Years*—set her among the cutting-edge leaders in the field. Her books have received enthusiastic reviews from Dr. Lucy Jane Miller and Lindsey Biel, MA, OTR/L. Britt presents her content nationwide alongside other experts, including Temple Grandin, Paula Aquilla, Diane Bahr, and Carol Kranowitz.

Britt's professional specialties include working with children with sensory processing disorder, autism spectrum disorder, ADHD, Down syndrome, feeding disorders, and more. Britt is also certified to teach yoga for children with special needs ages 0–12. She is working to complete her full yoga certification and her children's yoga certification.

Currently, Britt is practicing in Denver, Colorado, in the Cherry Creek School District. She also provides in-home early intervention for children ages birth to three through Results Matter Therapy. She and her husband are enjoying being new parents. For more information on Britt, please visit www.sensoryparenting.com and www.sensoryyogaforkids.com.

ABOUT THE ILLUSTRATOR

Carly Jo Hougen is an artist, yogi, and adaptive ski instructor from Eau Claire, Wisconsin. She has been drawing, painting, and photographing since she was a little girl. She has spent the last seven winters bouncing back and forth from Vail, Colorado to Minneapolis, MN to ski & snowboard with adults and children with special needs. Her clientele became her biggest inspiration—to turn her art into a career. She is currently a full-time artist and wedding photographer, and grateful for every opportunity to create. Her website is www.carlyjostudio.com.

OTHER TITLES BY BRITT COLLINS

WWW.SENSORYPARENTING.COM